EMOTION HACKS

Dr Ryan Martin

The Anger Professor

50 WAYS TO FEEL BETTER FAST

Emotion Hacks
Dr Ryan Martin

First published in the UK and USA in 2026 by Watkins,
an imprint of Watkins Media Limited
Unit 11, Shepperton House,
83–89 Shepperton Road
London N1 3DF

enquiries@watkinspublishing.com

Commissioning Editor: Fiona Robertson
Project Manager: Gigi St John
Head of Design: Karen Smith
Production: Uzma Taj

A CIP record for this book is available from the British Library

ISBN: 978-1-78678-867-2 (Paperback)
ISBN: 978-1-83681-017-9 (eBook)

10 9 8 7 6 5 4 3 2 1

Typset by Lapiz

Printed and bound by CPI Group (UK) Ltd, Croydon CR0 4YY

The manufacturer's authorised representative in the EU for
product safety is eucomply OÜ - Pärnu mnt 139b-14, 11317
Tallinn, Estonia, hello@eucompliancepartner.com;
www.eucompliancepartner.com

www.watkinspublishing.com

CONTENTS

*Dedicated to those
overwhelmed by emotion,
vulnerable in their hurt and
eager for a way forward.
This is for you.*

PART I
INTRODUCTION

CHAPTER 1
INTRODUCING THE HACKS TO FEEL BETTER FAST

Four Things I Would Never Do

In 2022, I shared a video on TikTok titled "Four Things I Would Never Do: Anger Edition." I was building off the "Four Things I Would Never Do" TikTok trend, where people of different professions shared things they would avoid based on their experiences in their work. For example, a relationship therapist would talk about the dangers of using the silent treatment, or an Intensive Care Unit nurse would talk about how she would never not wear a seatbelt. For my video, I shared four harmful ways of expressing anger, including (1) punching and breaking things as a way of blowing off steam, (2) voicing anger toward another driver while driving, (3) using exercise as a way of dealing with anger and (4) sending an email, text or posting on social media when angry.

People were a little surprised by number one (they like to believe that venting through the destruction of things is helpful), but they were really thrown by number three. Quite a few of them disagreed with me, arguing that exercise is the single best way to deal with emotions and telling me that they had been encouraged by their therapists to exercise when they were angry. For the record, and as I'll explain in more detail in Hack 11 (*see* page 66), the relationship between exercise and emotion is nuanced and complicated. Overall, exercise is good for your emotional wellbeing. But, exercising *when* you are angry (or scared) has a very different outcome to exercising as a way of preventing negative emotions.[1] As with everything, the details matter.

One person's response to this post really stood out. They said, "If exercise doesn't work, I'm really out of options here."

There were two reasons this comment jumped out at me. First, it was the lack of arguing or disagreement. They didn't say, "You're wrong, this is the only thing that works for me." They didn't say, "My therapist tells me to go punch a punching bag and it works great!" They just accepted that maybe this doesn't work and if it doesn't, they didn't know what else to do. There was a helplessness to the comment that I found troubling. Second, that this person couldn't find any other options for managing their emotional wellbeing was worrisome for me. There are a near-infinite number of little changes that can be made to our daily lives to considerably impact our emotional health. To think that someone felt so limited was really quite heartbreaking for me.

Small Changes, Big Impact

I have been researching people's experience of anger and other emotions for over 25 years now, and in addition to numerous academic research publications during that time, I have recently been reaching a more mainstream audience through my TED talk "Why We Get Mad – And Why It's Healthy" (now at over 3,600,000 views and counting), my social media channels and my two previous books, *Why We*

---

[1]   There's even been some research, published in *Circulation* (2016), that links angry exercise to an increased risk of heart attacks.

Get Mad (2021) and *How to Deal with Angry People* (2023). In all my research, writing, online videos and public speaking, my goal has always been to help people recognize the impact of subtle life changes on emotional wellbeing. I'm not trying to replace therapy or address significant mental health problems (though many of these adjustments can and should be included in therapy for such problems). I want to help people realize that small, easily achievable changes in their diet, sleep routine or ways of thinking – what I call "emotion hacks" – can affect their emotional life in demonstrable ways.

For example, take the findings of a 2023 study on the emotional impact of fragmented sleep,[2] which is where you're dealing with lots of brief wake-ups throughout the night. It is a little different from other forms of unhealthy sleep, because you're not going to bed too late or getting up too early; you're just not getting a good night's sleep because you keep waking up. This particular study confirmed something we've known for a while – that fragmented sleep has a negative impact on our mood – and it also explained *why*. The researchers found that a night of fragmented sleep increased our tendency to have negative thoughts the next day, with study participants being more likely to ruminate and self-criticize.

So, imagine the emotional impact of making some relatively subtle changes to sleep hygiene. By keeping your bedroom a little cooler and darker, by turning off screens an hour earlier or cutting back on your caffeine consumption[2] during the day, you can minimize that fragmented sleep in a way that has a powerful impact on your emotional health. A few straightforward adjustments, aka emotion hacks, can minimize the anger, sadness and anxiety you feel the next day, and improve your overall emotional life.

---

[2]   I may have just lost a lot of readers by suggesting they cut back on their coffee intake. "These were supposed to be *subtle* life changes, Ryan!"

It's Rarely One Big Thing

Learning to manage your emotions is rarely, if ever, going to be about doing one big thing. You can't necessarily plan on making one huge life change and expecting it to make all the difference. First, big life changes are difficult and often unsustainable. Second, big life changes frequently bring about a host of emotions, and not all of them are positive. For example, people will often anticipate happiness on the other side of some success, accomplishment or change in circumstances (e.g., "I'll be happy when I ... get a different job, move out, get married, get divorced," etc.). While it's true that those things may bring a certain level of happiness, especially in the short term, they also lead to stress, anxiety, frustration or other negative-feeling emotions. For example, that "better" job can bring with it stress and frustration associated with learning new skills, as well as anxiety over meeting and working with new people.

Instead, emotion management should be largely about developing lots of healthy emotional habits. Learn to take care of yourself physically (e.g., through exercise and sleeping and eating well), identify the provocations or threats you may unintentionally invite into your life, explore new ways of thinking or interpreting your day-to-day experiences, and other similar strategies. These types of changes, which are individually relatively small and easy to achieve, can lead to seismic shifts in the way you experience sadness, anger, fear, happiness and other emotions.

Two Important Caveats

I want to be very clear about two things at the outset. First, this book isn't designed to address serious and diagnosable emotional problems (e.g., major depressive disorder, generalized anxiety disorder). I don't want to minimize the severity of these serious medical conditions, which frequently require professional intervention, by suggesting they can be managed by simply getting a better night's sleep or exercising regularly. While the strategies outlined in the book might be helpful to people struggling with such diagnoses, they will probably be insufficient.

The second caveat is that I am well aware that not everyone has the luxury of being able to do the things outlined in this book. A healthy diet assumes access to healthy foods. A good night's sleep assumes a safe, secure and quiet sleeping space. These necessities are not available to everyone equally. One of the consequences of an unjust economic system is that it takes a toll not only on a person's physical health, but on their emotional and mental health too.

50 Research-Driven Strategies to Hack Your Emotions

I've organized this book in a specific way to help you get the most out of the suggestions I'm offering. Chapter 2 is designed to help you understand the science of how people experience emotions. I break down the process by which we feel things, explaining the triggers that tend to kick off an emotional experience, as well as what happens in our brain and body when we emote, and how what we do in those moments can influence the feeling itself.

Then we're straight into the useful, practical and exciting stuff: 50 research-driven emotion hacks for subtly shifting your day-to-day life. These emotion hacks are quick and easy yet rooted in scientific research, things you can implement immediately to feel better fast. By making simple intentional decisions – for example, to stay hydrated (*see* page 69) or spend time in nature (*see* page 73), avoid demandingness (*see* page 113) or keep things in perspective (*see* page 130) – you really can influence your emotions in positive ways.

The goal is not necessarily that you walk away remembering all 50 hacks. That would be unrealistic and likely unnecessary. In fact, I suspect you'll come across some ideas here that you already know and do successfully, so don't need to change. I want you to understand the big picture of how you feel things and to come away with some specific changes you can make to have a healthier and happier emotional life.

As most of you probably realize, we're living in challenging times. Political unrest, economic uncertainty and a recent global health crisis have many of us feeling emotionally overwhelmed. Those challenges are outside the control of most of us and leave us feeling powerless and anxious. But what we can control – what we do have power over – is how we navigate these difficult times. We can manage our day-to-day life in a way that makes us feel more secure and more comfortable; there are genuine ways of feeling better fast. These hacks really work and I urge you to try them – and to get in touch with me via @angerprofessor to let me know how you're doing with them.

CHAPTER 2
HOW AND WHY WE FEEL

"This crowd wants me to succeed"

In 2018, I did a TEDx talk in Fond du Lac, Wisconsin.[1] I knew that it would be one of the most important moments of my career, and I was terrified. I had spent months preparing. I had finalized my script more than a month before the talk and I had practiced it approximately five times per day, every day, for over a month. On the day, I tried to stay calm and probably looked it on the outside, but internally I was a wreck. There were about five talks before mine, so I spent the morning watching the other speakers. My thoughts were spiraling off in all sorts of nonsensical directions. "What if I blow it? What if I go blank? What if I pass out? What if I trip and fall down as I walk out there? What if I'm so nervous I throw up on stage?"

I wasn't nervous about public speaking. I had done that countless times and for much larger audiences. I was so nervous because I knew if this went well, it could be career changing. I wanted it to be perfect and I had put extraordinary pressure on myself to make it so.[2] When I was on deck to go next, I stood

---

[1]   I did it as a TEDx talk in 2018, but it was accepted by TED.com as an official TED talk in 2019.

[2]   It's not perfect, by the way. I think it's a good talk and I'm very

silently backstage while the person in front of me finished up. I could see the giant red clock getting closer and closer to 18 minutes, the maximum length of a talk, and I grew more and more anxious with each second. The speaker after me came and stood next to me, waiting for her turn. In an attempt to lighten the mood, she started making jokes. "Don't shit your pants out there," she said to me, probably not realizing that was already on my list of things that could go wrong.

I took the stage and started my talk to an eerily silent audience. I had been told to walk to the red circle, plant myself in a comfortable position, take a deep breath and start. I did exactly that. I was nervous and did what I could to keep my voice from shaking. Then, at exactly 30 seconds in, I made a little joke. It was barely a joke, honestly, and not something I really expected people to laugh at. But they did laugh, and some people even laughed sort of hard. In that moment, all my nervousness faded away. "This crowd wants me to succeed," I thought to myself, and I was instantly comfortable.

What *Is* an Emotion?

I'm sharing the above story because it nicely captures in real time the fascinating way in which emotions can work. It's rare that a thing just happens and *causes* a feeling. Emotions are usually the result of a confluence of situations, physiological states, thoughts and choices. They happen as a result of a variety of factors coming together, and we control some of those things more than we might realize. Having a healthy emotional life is about recognizing what parts of that pattern

---

proud of it, but one of the downsides of having practiced it so many times is that I'm acutely aware of how it *should* sound. Every time it doesn't sound the way I want it to, it's like fingernails on a chalkboard to me. Since it came out, I've only watched it one time from start to finish, and that's only because it was played at an event I was at and it would have been weird for me to get up and leave.

we have some control over and exerting that control when we can.

First, let's back up and answer a really important question: "What *is* an emotion?" This is a more complicated question than you might think. In fact, psychologists haven't come up with a single agreed-upon definition of an emotion. There are some psychologists, mostly behaviorists, who argue that emotions don't exist. Or, they believe they do exist but aren't really worth studying because they aren't observable. Another view is that emotions aren't a real category but are just the labels we give to a collection of distinct internal feeling states. My definition, and what this book will use, is that emotions are psychological states that include (1) physiological arousal, (2) a relatively predictable pattern of thoughts and (3) some common or expected behaviors (what we sometimes call "action tendencies").

So what does all that mean? Well, when we encounter a particular type of stimulus (spark) – let's say a spider – our heart rate might increase (physiological arousal), we might think, "It's going to bite me" (thought), and we might flee (behavior). Or, imagine learning that someone you like romantically also likes you that same way. With such a stimulus, there might be a rush of adrenaline giving you that feeling of your heart skipping a beat (physiological), you might think, "Oh thank God, they like me too" (thought), and you might allow yourself to move physically closer to them (behavior).

A couple of things to note. First, while every emotion includes these three elements, you might not be aware of them every time. There may be occasions when you have a feeling without necessarily identifying a thought about the stimulus or without noticing the physiology. I hear this about phobias relatively often. People tell me, "When I see a spider, I don't have a specific thought. I just get scared and want to get away from it."[3]

---

[3]   The startle response, which we often see connected to certain phobias, has a neurologically different origin to some other forms of

I've experienced this as well, particularly with fear. The emotional feeling comes on so quickly that it doesn't seem like there's a thought that pre-empts it. For example, I'm not a super comfortable flier, and when I'm on a plane and we hit turbulence or something like that, a moment of panic will hit quickly, before I've had the chance to articulate a thought. I would argue in those moments, though, that there is *some sort* of appraisal happening. It may be quick and ill-formed, but on some level I've thought, "We're going to crash!" Otherwise, why would I get scared?

The physiological arousal in those moments is relatively consistent. Our sympathetic nervous system kicks in (often called the "fight-or-flight response"), so our heart rate increases, our breathing becomes faster and deeper, we start to sweat and our digestive system slows down so our mouth goes dry. This is all geared toward preparing us to respond to a potential threat, injustice or loss. Rooted in our evolutionary history, this response provides us with the energy we need when we experience something dangerous or when someone or something tries to take something from us.

The third piece of the puzzle is our behavioral impulse, sometimes called an "action tendency." This is the behavior most often associated with the emotion. It's often what we *want* to do in these moments, and it's relatively predictable. When we're scared, we typically avoid the thing we're scared of. When we're angry, we may want to lash out at the person we're angry at. These are called "impulses" and "action *tendencies*," though, because we don't always act on them. We can be scared and approach the thing we're scared of. We can get angry without lashing out.

An important thing to realize here is that these behavioral

anxiety. For example, when you hear a loud noise or see/feel a thing you're afraid of, the startle response originates in the brainstem and sends messages to motor neurons which control your muscles to fire off a behavioral response. The reason you might not have a thought at first, then, is because you're bypassing the thought parts of the brain in favor of a speedy response.

impulses are often productive. Our emotions alert us to a need – they are motivators – and these behaviors exist to help fulfill that need. Our curiosity says, "There's information you don't know that could be important," and so we explore to learn that information. Our shame tells us, "You've done something wrong," and so we avoid eye contact and turn away from people to signal to them that we know we made a mistake.

Emotions, Thoughts and Behavioral Impulses

Emotion	Thought/appraisal	Behavioral impulses[4]
Fear	"That's dangerous."	Avoidance, flight
Anger	"That's not fair."	Lashing out physically or verbally
Sadness	"I've lost something important to me."	Crying, withdrawal
Joy	"This is pleasant."	Smiling, laughing
Curiosity	"This thing I don't know might be important."	Asking questions, exploring
Disgust	"That's gross."	Avoidance, refusal to touch something, cleaning
Shame	"I've done something terrible."	Avoiding eye contact, minimizing presence
Surprise	"That was unexpected and pleasant."	Jumping, orienting toward source of surprise
Jealousy	"I want what that person has."	Possessiveness, negative interactions with others
Pride	"I've done something impressive."	Boasting about achievements, standing taller

[4] People obviously don't always act on these behavioral impulses, but they often want to.

Why We Feel

When we emote, it's because three things (the initial stimulus, your mood and your interpretation) have come together in a particular way to produce an emotional feeling that led to an emotional expression. Moving forward, we're going to call this the Why We Feel Model. Its elements are:

1. **A stimulus:** This is the spark. It's a thing that happened, often but not always in your environment, that prompted the emotion.
2. **Your mood, defined broadly, at the time of that stimulus:** Are you tired, hungry, stressed, anxious, angry, physically uncomfortable or in some other mood that leads to an even more negative interpretation of the trigger?
3. **Your interpretation of that stimulus:** What this spark means to you. For you to emote, you have to decide if this thing is good or bad, fair or unfair, safe or dangerous, etc. You don't really emote in response to the stimulus, you emote in response to your interpretation of the stimulus.
4. **Emotional feeling:** The actual psychophysiological feeling state (e.g., joy, anger, sadness, fear, surprise, disgust, curiosity).
5. **Emotional expressions:** Any of the near-infinite behaviors that are activated by an emotion (e.g., crying, laughing, startling, swearing, journaling, assertion, aggression, smiling ...).

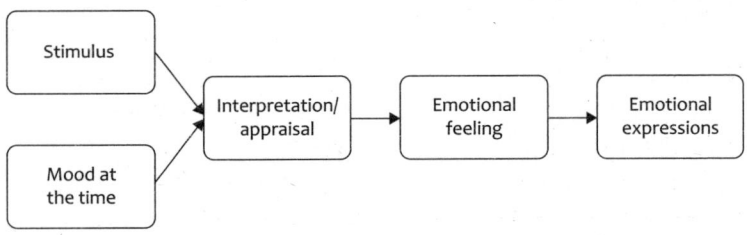

So, imagine you are driving to work one day. You had a late start and traffic is a little heavier than normal. Consequently, you're running late and you're starting to get anxious about making it to work on time. You are approaching a stoplight as it turns yellow. You think you can make it before it turns red, but the car in front of you stops for it, so you have to stop too. You think they are being overly cautious and now you're definitely going to be late for work. You get really angry at them for making you late.

What three elements have come together to lead to that anger?

- **The stimulus:** The driver in front of you not going through the light, so you have to stop.
- **Your interpretation:** The driver shouldn't have done that; you could have made it, now you're going to be late.
- **Your mood at the time:** Anxious about getting to work on time.

In this moment, the stimulus happens and you make an immediate appraisal about what it means to you in the context of your life and plans for that day. In this case, you decide its impact is negative and difficult for you to cope with – it will make you late for work. You may have had this emotional response regardless, but it's exacerbated by the fact that you were running late and already anxious. That nervousness leads to an even more negative appraisal of the trigger and that leads to even more intense anger.

This response, from stimulus to appraisal to emotional reaction, happens extraordinarily quickly. Neurologically, you take in information from your surroundings and your amygdala (a small structure deep in your brain responsible for initiating emotional responses) interprets the situation as angering and fires off messages to other parts of your brain. It simultaneously messages your hypothalamus to kick off your sympathetic nervous system response (your fight-or-flight response) and your facial motor nucleus to initiate an angry facial expression. Your heart rate increases, your muscles tense up, your breathing intensifies and you glare at the other driver. Next, your prefrontal cortex, the part of your brain that makes you most human, kicks in to help you think rationally about how you respond. You may honk, you may give the other driver the finger or you may decide that the safest course of action is to do nothing at all.

Hack Your Emotions

There's a 2002 article in *Psychophysiology* that I really like[i] by Dr. James J. Gross. He is a psychology professor at Stanford University, where he directs the Stanford Psychophysiology Laboratory, and he's an extraordinary scholar with approximately 600 publications to his name. What I like about this particular article is that it provides a nice framework to help us think about how we might regulate – or to use my word, hack – our own emotions. Gross starts by saying, "Emotion regulation refers to the processes by which we influence which emotions we have, when we have them, and how we experience and express them." Already, he's describing emotion regulation in much broader terms than most people tend to. For Gross, it's not a reactive process in which we respond to our emotions by trying to decrease them once we have them. Instead, it's about actually influencing the emotions we have in the first place, including when we have them, as well as what we do with them once we have them.

Gross highlights the difference between things we can do *before* the emotional response (what he calls "antecedent-focused strategies" and I am going to call "before-the-feeling strategies") and things we can do *after* the emotional response (what he calls "response-focused strategies" and I am going to call "after-the-feeling strategies).

Within this framework of before and after, Gross identifies five specific types of emotion-regulation strategies: four we do *before* the emotional response (situation selection, situation modification, attentional deployment and cognitive change) and one we do *after* the emotional response (response modulation).

- **Situation selection:** Where we choose our environments, making decisions about the situations we engage in.
- **Situation modification:** Where we adjust the situation, modifying the circumstances to alter its emotional impact.
- **Attentional deployment:** Where we direct our focus and select the specific elements of the situation that we pay attention to.
- **Cognitive change (reappraisal):** Where we rethink the meaning of situations and determine how we interpret the specific part of the situation we've paid attention to.
- **Response modulation:** Where we regulate our reaction, making specific attempts to influence the emotional response we have to the situation.

Returning to my TED talk as an example here, there were things I did before the talk that influenced my emotions: applying to talk in the first place (**situation selection**), practicing regularly to improve my performance (**situation modification**), choosing to ignore the jokes of my fellow speaker while backstage (**attentional deployment**), etc. As the anxiety built, I engaged in strategies to decrease it such as deep breathing and grounding myself (**response modulation**). The recognition in the moment that the crowd wanted me to succeed was a cognitive change that led to decreased anxiety and nervousness (**a reappraisal**).

If I'd made different decisions at each of these turns, I would have had wildly different emotional responses that day. I could have avoided the talk altogether. I could have chosen to practice less, leaving me less prepared. I could have focused even more on all the things that could go wrong or more readily engaged in jokes with the other speaker. I didn't have to think, "This audience wants me to succeed," and instead could have seen them as unsupportive or even antagonistic of my ideas.

Now, I didn't necessarily make these decisions with emotion regulation in mind. It's not as though I said, "By practicing I'll feel more prepared and less anxious on the day." I practiced because I wanted to do a good job. The point is that through the decisions I made, I was already hacking my own emotional responses. The choices I made before, during and after the talk influenced how I felt. More importantly, even though I wasn't always intentional about those things, I could have been. I could have been more aware of the links between what I did and the impact it would have on my emotions, and I could have acted intentionally to improve them.

That awareness and intentionality is what I want for you. It is why I wrote this book. That awareness and intentionality is how you hack your emotions. By thinking about the situations you select, how you can modify those situations, what you pay attention to, how you interpret your experiences and how you respond to those experiences, you can make a significant and meaningful impact on your emotional life.

Imagine a co-worker invites you to a party. You are friends with this co-worker but you haven't spent much time outside of work with them and you won't know many, if any, of the other party attendees. You're also someone who tends to be socially anxious, so this potential engagement is causing some nervousness. In the week leading up to the party, there are near-infinite decisions you can make that will have an impact on your emotional experience. For example, you can:

- decide if you even want to go (selection)
- decide to bring a friend with you (modification)
- ask your co-worker to introduce you to some of their friends in advance (modification)

- try to connect with some of your co-worker's friends on social media beforehand (modification).

And we can go on and on with these (e.g., decide to go for just an hour, tell your friend you're anxious and want them to introduce you to some people right away so you have someone to talk with, look up and practice strategies for introducing yourself at a party, get there right away so you have time to get comfortable before a lot of people arrive, get there late when there are lots of guests there so you can more easily blend in and not be the center of attention).

At the party, you can choose what to pay attention to (attentional deployment). If engaging with people is causing anxiety, you can shift your focus to the environment, paying attention to how the home is decorated, the music that's playing or the food and drink options. You can intentionally engage in people-watching, to take your focus off yourself.[5] You can choose either to participate in activities or not to participate in activities, depending on how this might influence your mood.

Once you've decided what to pay attention to, you can decide how to interpret those things (cognitive change). Maybe you notice a group of people laughing. You can interpret that laughter in quite a few different ways. Maybe someone in the group is particularly funny. Maybe it's nervous laughter from a group of similarly anxious partygoers. Maybe they're laughing at you. Each of these interpretations is going to lead to a different set of emotions and perhaps even some possible strategies for how you engage. If someone in that group is funny, maybe that's a good group to join as a way of giving you a distraction from your nervousness.

---

[5]   This tip is only relevant to particular people but ... if the party host has a dog, find their dog. For dog people, there are few better ways to deploy your attention at a party than to distract yourself with a dog.

Finally, you can identify ways to manage your emotional responses as you have them (response modulation). When you find yourself getting tense, you can take a few deep breaths; you can ground yourself by identifying things you can see, hear and feel. You can count to ten in your head. You can find a quiet place to regroup for a moment before you go back to the party. Each of these quick approaches will help you scale back your anxiety in the moment by decreasing your arousal.

It's All About Context

I'm sometimes asked what the *best* approach is for managing emotions. The truth is, there isn't a single best approach. The best thing to do is always contextual. Hacking your emotions is about understanding why an emotion is occurring in a specific situation and intervening in any or all of the stages described in the Why We Feel Model. Sometimes emotion regulation is about anticipating future emotions and approaching the situation in the best possible way for your emotional life. And sometimes, emotion regulation is simply about taking good care of yourself so that even unanticipated life experiences are emotionally manageable.

So, how can you regulate any anger you might have in the driving example (see page 15)? This is fundamentally different from the anxiety you felt about going to a party. You knew the party was coming and had a week to prepare for it. What do you do with a completely unexpected situation – one that leaves you a little bit helpless and very frustrated?

We can start by thinking of it in terms of Gross's antecedent-focused strategies (the things we can do *before* a stimulus). In this case, though, because the trigger was unexpected, it's helpful to separate out the things you can't control (the unexpected traffic) from the things you can control (your reaction to the unexpected traffic).[6] By engaging in some stress-management approaches as you drive (Hacks 6, 37, etc.), you decrease the tension you'll feel when you encounter a traffic jam or someone else's bad driving (situation modification to improve your mood at the time of the trigger).

You can also intervene in this situation with your interpretation of the stimulus. When you were stopped, you engaged in what emotion researchers often call "other-directed-shoulds" ("The other driver shouldn't have done this; they're being overly cautious"; *see* Hack 24) and maybe some catastrophizing ("Now I'm going to be late for work"; *see* Hack 19). It's possible these things are true. Perhaps this person really was being too cautious and maybe you are now going to be late for work. It's also worth considering other explanations or interpretations (Hack 18). Is it fair, for example, to label their behavior as overly cautious? Maybe your lateness made you more willing to take risks than usual. Or, consider how much time you *really* lost because of this. What will the consequences actually be for that kind of delay? If this doesn't work, you can try other types of reappraisal strategies (e.g., Hacks 27, 28, 29 and 30). These kinds of approaches can help you work through your feelings and better manage your emotional reactions.

Finally, you can manage the emotion itself once it happens (response-focused emotion regulation). When you get angry at the delay, you can take immediate steps to de-escalate your negative-feeling emotions. There are about ten different forms of deep breathing that can be effective here (e.g., triangle, box, belly, pursed-lip, alternate-nostril breathing; *see* Hack 40). You can also take a moment for a quick guided

---

[6]   Technically, you can also control your late departure, which caused the stress that exacerbated the angry response. But bringing that up felt a little victim-blaming ... especially for so early in the book. I'll wait until we've developed a closer relationship before I start scolding you for your lack of punctuality.

visualization to help you relax[7] (Hack 42) or develop a mantra to use in those sorts of moments. You can also decide what you do with the emotion. Do you assert yourself? Are you aggressive? Do you do nothing? Do you drive faster and more dangerously once the light turns green? We are faced with a multitude of choices when we emote, and what we decide to do in those moments is important.

Build Your Emotion Hackpack

Healthy emotion management requires two things: (1) a comprehensive understanding of how and why you are experiencing your feelings and (2) a variety of strategies, or hacks, you can employ as interventions when you identify feelings you want to experience differently. In this chapter, I've laid out a framework with which you can develop that comprehensive understanding. The hope is that you can take any emotional experience and unpack it using the Why We Feel Model. To help you use the model, start with the following four questions.

1. What's the emotion?
2. What's the stimulus and how did I interpret that stimulus?
3. What was my mood at the time of the stimulus?
4. How did I express this emotion?

The rest of the book will focus on the second part of emotional management, providing 50 hacks you can use to intervene in all stages of the emotional experience. Put the strategies that appeal to you in your hackpack (like a backpack, but for hacks), to be implemented when the situation calls for it.

[7]   People often react to this by saying, "There's not enough time for that when you're just stuck at a stoplight." If that's true and there's not enough time for a simple visualization exercise, then how bad can this delay actually be?

There will be times when a situation needs reappraisal, when the best thing to do is pause and ask yourself if your initial interpretation is correct or productive. There will be other times when you need to stop inviting particular triggers into your life. On other occasions, it is rest, exercise or a healthier diet that is needed most.

Too often we think of emotion management as being about decreasing unwanted emotions, but it's much more than simply reducing our anger, sadness or fear. Emotion management includes finding ways to increase wanted emotions such as joy, curiosity or excitement. It also involves recognizing that some situations may call for emotions that have traditionally been considered negative. There is a time and place for anger, sadness and fear, and emotion management is about being able to identify that time and place while having the tools to bring those emotions to the surface.

PART II
THE EMOTION HACKS

CHAPTER 3
BIG PICTURE HACKS

The 50 emotion hacks in this book are categorized based on where they fit into the Why We Feel Model (*see* page 14): the stimulus, your mood at the time of the stimulus, your interpretation of that stimulus, the emotional feeling and the emotional expression.

First, though, there are three emotion hacks that don't fit into a specific stage of the model. Rather, they reflect a way of understanding the broader picture of why you in particular feel things the way you do. Remember, when you emote it's because three things came together – a trigger, your mood and your interpretation of the trigger – to create that emotional feeling. And from that emotional feeling comes some sort of emotional expression. This is true of both positive-feeling emotions and negative-feeling emotions.[1]

For example, imagine you're a student and you earn a B+ on an exam (stimulus). That will feel very different depending on how you interpret that grade. If you believe you're capable of earning an A in the class (interpretation), a B+ will feel disappointing and you might get sad (emotional feeling).

---

[1] I try really hard not to fall into the trap of thinking of some emotions as positive and others as negative because all emotions are meaningful and important to pay attention to. But the truth is that some emotions tend to feel better than others. Some tend to be wanted (e.g., joy, contentment) and some tend to be unwanted (e.g., sadness, guilt). So, I'll refer to them as negative or positive as that's how they are commonly referred to. Please try to remember that even though some emotions don't typically feel good, that doesn't necessarily make them negative.

But if you were just hoping for a C or better, a B+ means you exceeded your expectations (interpretation) and you'll feel happy.

In this chapter, we'll discuss the importance of paying attention to the overall picture of how your emotions are generated. I'll outline three strategies for exploring that big picture, including:

- Hack 1: Diagram the Emotion
- Hack 2: Identify Your Emotional Patterns
- Hack 3: Log Your Moods

These three emotion hacks will help you better understand how and why you feel things, which in turn will help you recognize which of the later hacks will be most important to develop and use.

Hack 1: Diagram the Emotion

Unbelievably Slow Fast-Food

There is a very popular "fast-food" chain here in Wisconsin.[2] The food is good, they have great ice cream, my kids love it and every time I go there, I regret it. Why? Because they're unbelievably slow. About a week ago, I was bringing my son home from soccer practice and we decided to stop there. It was a little late in the evening, so I foolishly thought I had avoided the evening rush and would be fine. I was wrong. I'm not exaggerating when I say that it took me 15 minutes to get from the intercom where I ordered the food to the window where I paid for the food. And the food wasn't ready when I got there, so I had to park and wait another 15 minutes. Finally, I got my order and headed home for what was now going to be a very late dinner. When I got there and unpacked the bag, I discovered they had not included two of the three sandwiches I ordered. I got really, really mad.

Explore Your Feelings

Take a moment to think about an occasion like this when you were really emotional. For simplicity, pick a situation when you were feeling just one thing, such as anger, sadness or fear.[3] Now, break it down and identify the different

---

[2]   We're going to put "fast-food" in quotes because ... it's not fast. That's the whole point of the story. It's a very, very slow-food restaurant.

[3]   We often feel multiple things at the same time, and that's because we interpret situations in lots of different ways and those situations can have lots of different meanings for us. A friend getting a great job may lead to happiness (*"Good for them"*), jealousy (*"They sure have their life together in ways I don't"*) and even anxiety (*"What if this takes them away from me?"*).

elements using the Why We Feel Model (*see* page 14). What was:

- the stimulus?
- your mood at the time of the stimulus?
- your interpretation of the stimulus?
- the emotional feeling?
- your expression of that emotion?

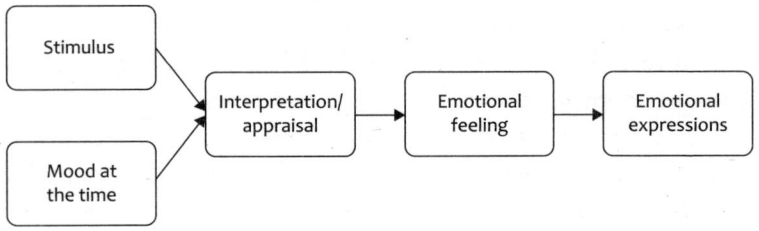

For each of these questions, you need to be specific. The stimulus isn't what was going on all day leading up to the emotion. It's the specific thing that you reacted to (e.g., learning your favorite athlete got traded, having a near car accident). In my case above, the trigger was discovering I didn't get the right food. Were there other frustrations? Yes. But when you diagram an emotional incident, you want to be specific about the spark.

What about that other stress and frustration I was experiencing? Those feelings were part of my mood at the time of the stimulus. I was feeling a combination of stressed, tired, frustrated and uncomfortable from having sat in the car for so long,[4] and that mood undoubtedly influenced my interpretation of the stimulus. That interpretation was a combination of other-directed-shoulds ("All that time and they didn't even get it right") and catastrophizing

---

[4]   If we wanted to, we could diagram each of these other feeling states. Waiting so long could be considered as the stimulus that I then interpreted in a way that led to frustration. These stimuli and appraisals build on one another over time.

("Now what are my kids going to eat? Going back to get our food is going to be such a pain"). The emotional feeling was anger and I expressed it by swearing to myself and then immediately trying to problem solve … in a way that didn't require me to go back to the restaurant.

Know When to Intervene

I recommend diagramming your emotional incidents any time you feel something even relatively strongly. I know that might seem like a lot to do when you're emoting, but you get better and faster at it as you practice. For me, now, it just happens habitually.

Why do it? Two reasons. First, because it's an immediate step to identify where you can intervene. By breaking down the situation into its component parts, you can identify different options for how you can better manage your emotions, both proactively and in response. For example, in this case, it tells me both what I *could* have done differently (avoided this restaurant at a time when I was feeling rushed and tired) and what I *can* now do in the midst of my anger (reframe my appraisal and find ways to stay calm while I problem solve).

The second reason is that diagramming emotional incidents this way helps you identify patterns. Over time, I'll be able to recognize particular mood states, triggers and interpretations that I tend to engage in. Understanding those patterns is critical to hacking your emotions.

Hack 2: Identify Your Emotional Patterns

Unexpected Anxieties

I used to work at a college counseling center where one of my responsibilities was to be on call after hours. On the surface, it was simple. I carried a pager[5] around and if it went off, I called a number and was connected to a student who was in some form of distress. In practice, it was really stressful. The pager didn't go off very often – less than once a night – but when it did go off, there was usually a lot to do and it might take hours and include hospital visits, calls to the police or seeking the involvement of other emergency care providers.

For about four months, I did this every Thursday night from 5pm to 8am on Friday morning.[6] After that, though, we switched up the schedule so I was working on Wednesday nights instead of Thursday nights. That first Thursday night after the schedule changed, something fascinating happened. At around 4pm, I found myself feeling anxious.

I had nothing to be anxious about. I had done my on-call duty the night before, but as I sat in my office finishing up my day, I started to feel nervous. At first I couldn't place where the nervousness was coming from. It wasn't intense, just a low-grade feeling of anxiety that I couldn't entirely explain. But then it hit me: I was so used to Thursdays being my on-call night that my brain and body were reacting to that history. My anxiety wasn't rooted in what was actually happening in the moment but in the pattern that had developed over the last few months.

5   Yup ... this was a long time ago. To see a person with a pager meant that they were important and I felt super cool having one hooked on my belt. I cringe just thinking about it now.

6   There was nothing so relieving as having the clock hit 8am those mornings ... and nothing quite as disheartening as when the pager went off after 7:30am.

The Importance of Understanding Patterns

My on-call experience might be an unusual example, but it speaks to a broader set of phenomena. Our emotions are reactive to patterns in our daily life. We might find ourselves a little frustrated on Sunday nights because our work week is right around the corner. We might start to feel down more regularly in late fall because the holidays are coming and that's a stressful time for us.

These patterns aren't just related to timing but might also be associated with specific people or activities. Even fun activities that you're looking forward to might bring out unexpected anxieties that drive a pattern of discomfort. For example, despite all the fun of travel, it brings with it a certain amount of stress and worry. People regularly find themselves irritable and frustrated as they approach a vacation without fully understanding why. In the moment, they simply fail to recognize their anxiety, even as it impacts them physically and emotionally.

A parent once shared with me that her seven-year-old son would get really crabby whenever he visited his grandparents. For the first evening of every visit, he was irritable. A normally fun and lighthearted kid, he would act out in ways that were unusual. As we talked about it, it became evident that the son was dealing with two different anxieties that were leading to that crabbiness. First, even though he liked visiting his grandparents, being away from his home made him uncomfortable. He missed his room. He missed his toys. He felt out of place at his grandparents, and that discomfort led to irritability. Second, being around his grandfather put the son on edge. His grandfather tended to be strict, so even though he loved his grandfather and enjoyed spending time with him, there was a certain amount of anxiety that came with those visits. He got anxious about doing something wrong and getting in trouble. That anxiety drove some irritability directed at his parents and siblings.

The Power of Awareness

Take a moment right now and ask yourself three questions.

1. What are the recurring triggers (stimuli) that lead to strong emotions from you?
2. How do you usually feel in those moments (e.g., what emotion do you typically have)?
3. What themes do you notice in those triggers?

The last question might be the most important. You may find that feeling powerless is the common theme that leads to a variety of strong feelings. Or, you may find that feeling unnoticed or unrecognized is the theme.

Regardless, identifying these patterns can help you in two ways. First, simply being aware on its own makes a difference. Recognizing that you get sad in the fall or anxious or frustrated on Sunday nights alone is an intervention. Now, when you start to feel down, you at least have an explanation and that relieves the uncertainty and gives you a sense of control. When I discovered my anxiety was rooted in my previous on-call schedule, everything shifted for me. The anxiety started to dissipate immediately because I realized it was caused by something that was no longer relevant.

The second way it can help is that it allows for better ways of dealing with the issue. When that parent realized the origin of her son's irritability, it helped her approach the situation differently. She became more patient with him, asked his grandfather to lighten up, and made a point of giving her son extra time and space on that first night of the visit. She would take him aside when they got there and tell him that if he needed to be by himself for a few minutes to get acclimated, he could. Understanding the pattern – getting a picture of what was really going on – suggested a set of healthy interventions that shifted her son's emotional wellbeing.

Hack 3: Log Your Moods

Monitor Your Emotions to Shift Your Feelings

In 2021, three researchers from the University of Warwick published an article on the value of mobile mood monitoring.[ii] They asked 47 participants, approximately half with mental health problems and half without, to use a mood-monitoring app for three weeks. The app they used, Catch It,[7] asks you to record and reflect on your mood; and all the participants had to do for the study was log their mood twice a day. Before and after those three weeks, participants took surveys on emotion regulation and general health. What the researchers found was that the participants experienced a significant decrease in the intensity of their negative moods during the three weeks. The mere act of monitoring emotions, without being asked to do anything differently to manage those emotions, led to a shift in how those feelings were experienced.

The researchers also interviewed a subset of those same participants to gain additional information about what the experience was like for them. The researchers found that using the app led to more honest conversations between the participants and their therapists, and that increased self-awareness led to better mood management; the researchers also saw that labeling emotions led to improved emotional language and a decrease in impulsive behaviors. Taken together, this study really shows the value of keeping track of your feelings. By paying attention to emotions and logging them, you develop a healthier emotional life.

---

[7] I had to know if this app came out before or after the Covid-19 health crisis, and it turns out it launched in 2014. I'm glad because naming an app "Catch It" during or after a pandemic seems like poor judgment.

Though the technology is relatively new, the concept of mood logging or mood journaling has been around for a long time.[8] In fact, a mood log is a common practice in therapy because it's a great way to help people develop a better understanding of their emotions. Therapists will ask their clients to take a mood log home with them for a week and fill it out at the end of each day (e.g., identify and label any strong emotions you might have had, rate the intensity of those emotions). The client brings the log back to the next session and they go over the results together.

The great thing about a mood log like this is that it allows you to focus on what you most need to focus on. So, if your particular concern is the thoughts you have when you're emotional, you can keep track of that. You can even list alternative thoughts you could have had that would have led to a different emotional response. Or if your concern is the types of provocations that tend to lead to a particular emotion, you can keep special track of that instead. You can start to pay attention not just to specific situations but to broader categories of situations (e.g., situations when I feel unheard, situations when I feel helpless).

Why Does Mood Logging Work?

Why does emotion tracking like this work to help manage your emotions? It does a few things for you. First, a mood log can be a critical tool when it comes to identifying those patterns that are so important to understand (see Hack 2). For example, learning that you are more likely to get anxious when you're fatigued can help you prevent future anxiety by encouraging you to stay well rested when you can.

---

[8] A student once showed me a mood journal she had been given by her parents. It was a fascinating tool because it encouraged tracking mood in all sorts of creative and clever ways. It wasn't just a mood log but provided prompts on thoughtful topics such as "What are you grateful for today?" and "How did your sadness feel?"

A mood log or mood journal like this can give you the information you need to identify those patterns. It's one of the ways you can determine your emotional tendencies regarding the situations and also the thoughts and moods that tend to bring out your emotions.

Second, just paying attention to your emotions can have an impact on how you experience them. Noticing your anger can lead to a decrease in anger. Acknowledging your sadness can lead to a decrease in that sadness. In fact, rating the intensity of your emotions in the moment can be a valuable way to manage them.[9] What you sometimes realize is that your emotions aren't nearly as intense as you thought. Or you may realize that even when they are intense, they aren't that long lasting.

What I love about this approach is that it's customizable and simple. You can use an app, buy a journal, download one of the many mood logs you can find for free online or make your own. All you really need to do is start paying attention, logging regularly and maybe taking some time to reflect on your findings. You don't need to spend more than a few minutes each day, but the time you do spend can offer a lot of insight and value.

[9] I do this when I fly. If I find myself getting anxious, I rate that anxiety on a scale of 1 to 10. Doing so helped me realize that my anxiety wasn't nearly as long lasting as I thought it was. I would have guessed I was at level 10 for the entire flight, but what I found was that level 10 anxious feelings were rarer than I thought, and there were plenty of times when I wasn't very anxious at all.

CHAPTER 4
STIMULUS HACKS

Whenever you get scared, surprised, happy, sad, angry or any other feeling, you can likely identify some sort of trigger. You got happy because you got a new job. You got scared because you saw a spider. You got curious because you saw a clickbait headline on social media. These triggers are often perceived to be outside our control. They are things we think happen to us instead of things we can change.

That might be true some of the time, but ultimately we have a lot of control over the stimuli we face each day. We can prevent, modify and manipulate the triggers we experience. We may have to drive to work each day, but we can select what time we leave, what route we take, what we listen to along the way and a bunch of other elements of the experience. We may have to give a speech in a class we're taking, but we can decide how much we prepare for that speech. Each of those decisions might change how we experience that stimulus (or even whether we experience that stimulus at all). Getting stopped by a red light is far more frustrating when you're running late, and giving a speech is far more anxiety-provoking when you haven't prepared.

In this chapter, I'll talk about how we can affect our emotions by making intentional decisions about the triggers we face each day. I'll provide five different strategies for how we can be thoughtful about the situations we engage in, including how to manipulate them or distract ourselves when necessary.

- Hack 4: Select Situations Wisely
- Hack 5: Take Control of Situations
- Hack 6: Embrace Healthy Distraction
- Hack 7: Mind Your Memories
- Hack 8: Harness Your Imagination

The goal here isn't to avoid things that are scary or angering, and it's certainly not to try to participate only in situations that make us feel good. The goal is to embrace a thoughtful and intentional approach to how we engage with the world.

Hack 4: Select Situations Wisely

Inviting Fear into My Life

About 15 years ago, I watched a horror movie that had me up all night afterwards. I wasn't that scared when I was watching it, but some of the images and ideas lingered in a way that was really upsetting to me. As I tried to sleep, I kept having these intrusive thoughts and the images popping into my head made it impossible for me to fall or stay asleep. The next day, exhausted and frustrated, I said to myself, "This is dumb. Don't do this to yourself anymore. You're just not cut out for horror movies, so don't go see them."[1]

I'm guessing this story resonates with a lot of people who simply do not like the way horror movies make them feel so they choose to avoid them. Athough, what doesn't usually resonate with people is how they can use that exact same principle with other areas of their life. If you can avoid horror movies because they scare you, you can also avoid other things that make you feel scared or sad or angry, etc.

This is but one example of that situation selection I discussed in the introduction. In your day-to-day life, you can make decisions about at least some of the stimuli you engage with. You can decide if you want to spend time consuming particular media or being in particular environments or even being with particular people. In fact, you're already doing that regularly, but you can be more intentional about the emotional impact of those decisions.

Here's another example. As I write this, we're in the middle of a divisive election season in the United States, and

---

[1]   This is relatively common for people as they age. They start to prioritize positive emotions because life is short and they don't want to invite negative feelings into their life. It's called "socioemotional selectivity" and it's one of the reasons why horror movies, amusement parks and haunted houses are more popular with young people.

I am choosy about how I engage with politics. I'm not saying I don't engage in politics. I do. I vote. I donate. I even volunteer regularly. But what I don't do is consume much political media. I don't watch political ads, I avoid political news programming and I don't watch the election returns come in on election night. Once I've made my decision regarding who to vote for, I avoid as much information as possible. When what seems like critical news breaks, I inevitably hear about it, so I go to a trusted news source and I learn what I need to learn.

It's not that I don't care. In fact, it's the opposite. I care too much and that sort of media isn't good for me. It offers me nothing positive and takes a real toll on my psychological wellbeing. Much like watching a horror movie, too much political content damages my emotional health, leaving me scared, angry and sad.

Now, I know there's at least someone reading right now who's thinking, "Being able to avoid politics comes from privilege. The rest of us have to pay attention because the outcomes could be life or death." So, I want to be clear that I'm not avoiding politics. I'm being mindful of the specific parts of political conversations that I choose to engage with. I'm making sure I get the information that I need to make an informed decision and then I'm opting out of any further information.

Don't Get Stuck in Your Comfort Zone

It's possible for us to be specific and intentional about a variety of situations we opt into or out of. For example, if you are prone to road rage, you can be thoughtful about how often you drive and the situations in which you drive (e.g., embracing public transportation, car pools or finding other routes to work with less traffic). If you find yourself immersed in negativity at work, you can make a point of scheduling time with positive people throughout your day, opting into environments where you feel happier or more comfortable. If you find crowds overwhelming or stressful, you can decide to shop at less busy times to mitigate that anxiety and stress.

There is a danger in this approach, though, that you need to be careful of. First, of course, not every situation can be avoided (we're going to talk about that with Hack 5). Second, as a general rule, avoidance leads to further or even increased discomfort. For example, as a pattern, avoiding a spider because you are afraid of that spider results in future avoidance, which means you never overcome your fear of spiders. The same thing could happen to someone with an issue with large crowds (or me with politics). If you keep avoiding the thing you're uncomfortable with, you don't give yourself an opportunity to get over that discomfort.

This is why you need more than one hack in your emotional wellness hackpack. You need to be able to know if it's OK to avoid something some of the time and have other strategies in place for those things you want to avoid but shouldn't. You need to understand how emotions occur so that you can tell when an approach that feels good in the short term might not be so good for you in the long run.

Hack 5: Take Control of Situations

Modification, Distraction or Reappraisal

There's not a lot of research on how well before-the-feeling (antecedent-focused) strategies work. Does situation selection actually lead to improved mood? Is situation modification something people use regularly and does it have a positive impact?[2] Does one strategy work better than the other? The theory and logic behind such approaches is sound and makes sense, so we know they *should* work. But what does the research say?

However, a 2020 article in *Motivation and Emotion*[iii] investigated some of these questions, and did so in a really interesting way. The researchers wanted to know how people used situation modification, distraction and reappraisal to regulate their emotions. To do so, they presented participants with pairs of negative pictures, some mildly upsetting (e.g., a minor car accident) and some intensely upsetting (e.g., a picture of a car crash with visible injuries). Participants then chose between three different emotion-management approaches.

- **Situation modification:** Participants could choose to fade out part of one of the pictures so they didn't have to look at it.
- **Distraction:** Participants could ask to have their focus guided to a more neutral part of the picture.
- **Reappraisal:** Participants could ask for a sentence to help reinterpret the more upsetting picture.

---

[2]   In a profoundly unscientific "study," I asked my social media followers how intentional they were in considering the emotional impact of situations they select, and a surprising number said "very" (28 per cent) or "moderately" (35 per cent). At the same time, though, 16 per cent said "not at all."

The researchers found a couple of really interesting outcomes here. First, participants were relatively good at using these approaches to manage their emotions to effectively decrease their distress. Second, participants preferred distraction or modification when the pictures were more intense, but they would turn to reappraisal for milder images.

I think this implies that it's hard to reappraise an intensely negative situation in a more positive way, so trying to distract yourself from it is more productive. In other words, if you see a really bad car accident, telling yourself, "An ambulance is on the way" probably won't undo the emotional distress, so it's better to look away or think about something else. But if you see a minor car accident, knowing an ambulance is on the way might be enough to make you feel better.[3]

Putting It into Practice

How then do we employ the above strategies in a real-life context, out of the research lab? If we don't want to avoid situations in the way we talked about in Hack 4, but we do want to approach them in a different way, what do we do? Ultimately, situation modification is about finding strategies that will allow you to engage with upcoming triggers (e.g., events, activities, conversations) in a way that will enable you to feel what you hope to feel.

This is likely something you're already doing on some level, either intentionally or unintentionally. For example, you've probably brought a friend to a party because you thought it would be more fun for you to have them there. It's common and natural to want to take steps to change your

---

[3]   If there's one point I'm going to try to hammer home all book long, it's this: healthy emotion management requires lots of different skills and approaches. This article reveals exactly that. The participants needed different strategies for different situations.

environment in a way that helps you feel more comfortable. What I'm suggesting here, though, is to take time and put effort into making those decisions intentionally.

For example, imagine you're going to your in-laws for a holiday dinner and you're feeling anxious about it. In the past, your in-laws haven't been very kind to you and they hold opinions you find offensive. If avoiding that situation doesn't feel like an option to you, here are a few things you can do to modify the situation in your favor, lessening both the anxiety leading up to the dinner and the discomfort during the dinner.

- Plan your arrival and departure times in advance. This will give a finish line to focus on when things get uncomfortable. It will also help you and your partner stay on the same page regarding plans, eliminating that potential stressor.
- Engage in some pre-event relaxation. This will modify the situation by decreasing some of the nervousness you might be feeling as you head into the party.
- Communicate with your partner or your in-laws in advance. You can reach out to your in-laws in advance of the dinner to let them know there might be things you don't want to discuss when you're there.
- Prepare some conversation starters or topic changers. Take some time to prepare for when conversations go in a direction you don't like, such as simple statements you can make to shift the topic to something else.

Each of these ideas is a relatively quick and easy yet empowering approach you can take to manage an emotionally complicated situation through modification.

Hack 6: Embrace Healthy Distraction

"Look for the helpers"

There's a famous quote from Fred Rogers that many of you have probably heard before: "When I was a boy and I would see scary things in the news, my mother would say to me, 'Look for the helpers. You will always find people that are helping.'"[iv]

Now, I want to proceed cautiously here because when I looked up this quote just now, I unexpectedly came across a number of think-pieces on how it is problematic. Most notably is an *Atlantic* article from 2018 by Ian Bogost titled, "The Fetishization of Mr. Rogers's 'Look for the Helpers,'" which argues that the quote was intended as a strategy to comfort children in the wake of tragedies, but is bad advice for adults and should make us as a society uncomfortable.[v] The quote, Bogost says, has been co-opted to avoid taking substantive action to solve social problems.

I think this argument is fair overall, and so I want to be clear at the outset that I'm not suggesting distraction as an *all-the-time approach*. Like situation selection and situation modification,[4] distraction is a *sometimes* approach.

Embracing Distraction

My dad died in 2020 during the Covid-19 pandemic. He was in an assisted living facility more than a thousand miles away from me. My mom and siblings were spread out across the country at a time when we weren't traveling (or even really leaving the house regularly). He died on a Sunday. I logged into work on Monday. I didn't have anything else to do that day, and I wanted the distraction.

---

[4]   And ice cream. Ice cream is also a sometimes approach.

I know some people will have balked when they read that just now. It feels wrong to be at work the day after losing your dad. And I could tell by my co-workers' faces that they were surprised to see me and some even questioned if I should be there. It felt to people like denial or suppression, but it wasn't. I spent part of the day crying and other parts writing about my dad. I went for a long walk with my dog and listened to my dad's favorite music along the way. I looked through pictures of him and took time to share stories with my family over Zoom. I also wanted breaks from those feelings and distracting myself with work was one of the ways I did that.

Not Just OK, but Healthy

Revisiting the 2020 article from *Motivation and Emotion* that we looked at in Hack 5 – about how people use situation modification, distraction and reappraisal to regulate their emotions – reveals that distraction does indeed regulate emotions. That study found that participants could successfully use distraction as a way of dealing with intense negative emotions. When the participants saw an upsetting photo, they would sometimes ask to be guided away from the upsetting part of the image and toward a more neutral part. What makes this interesting to me, especially in light of Bogost's response to Rogers's quote, is that this was a situation where there was no option to take substantive action. There was nothing the participant could do to solve the problem in the picture, just as there was nothing I could do to bring my dad back to life. In such cases, some distraction isn't just an OK option, it's a healthy one.

Again, this strategy is rooted in the idea that one approach to managing emotions is selecting specific elements of a situation to pay attention to (attentional deployment, *see* page 17). You can do this both in an emotional moment and by planning ahead for expected emotional moments. For example:

- Bring a favorite book with you on a flight, so you can immerse yourself in something comfortable and safe at a time when you might be scared or stressed.
- Play video games or listen to music when you're feeling down to focus your mind on something different from the sadness.
- Go for a walk in nature and be intentional about engaging with the natural world through birdwatching or identifying plants.
- Allow yourself to get lost in a movie or TV show when you want a break from reality.
- Engage in a hobby such as gardening or knitting as a means of expressing yourself and disengaging temporarily from other parts of life.

Such distractions not only allow you to avoid some uncomfortable emotions when it's appropriate but can also energize you. The world can feel really overwhelming sometimes, so some distraction from the difficult parts can be healthy.

Hack 7: Mind Your Memories

Actual, Imagined and Recollected Anger

In 1999, three researchers set out to establish how angry they might be able to make people in the lab.[vi] While it sounds a little pathological, being able to induce emotions is really important for research. If you want to study what someone is like when they're angry, sad, scared or guilty, you need to get them into that state while they're in a place where they can be studied.

The researchers' goal was to determine if any differences existed between various types of mood-induction procedures. In the lab, they hooked up participants to devices that would assess skin resistance (essentially a test of how much they sweat) and heart rate. Participants were told to relax for eight minutes while the devices took measurements of their physiological activation. Participants were then given one of three sets of instructions. The first two groups were told either to *imagine* a situation that would make them mad or to *remember* a past event that made them mad. The third group, labeled the "actual anger" group, was abruptly told that a mistake had been made, that the experiment couldn't continue and that they wouldn't receive compensation for attending the study. They were then ignored for the next 30 seconds, even as they asked questions or voiced frustration.

Because the researchers were gathering skin-conductance and heart-rate data, they could assess how each type of provocation and poor treatment might lead to an increase in sweating and heart rate. There were two interesting findings. First, just *remembering* an angering event led to physiological activation. Second, physiological symptoms were far more intense in the first two groups than in the "actual anger" group, even though the latter were the only participants who were actually treated poorly and provoked right there in the lab.

On a related note, four years later the authors did the same study, utilizing the same method, but with mirth.[vii] And they found essentially the same thing. Recollected mirth led to a much more intense physiological response than was seen in the "actual mirth" group.[5]

Memories Make Us Mad and Mirthful

The above-mentioned research is one of my favorite psychological studies about anger.[6] I like it both because I find the method used really creative and interesting, and because the results – that remembering an angry incident from the past led to a more intense physiological response than being provoked in the moment – aren't what a lot of people expect.

To be clear, I'm certain (and I suspect this is true of the mirth version as well) that a big part of what was going on in this study was that the moment from the participants' past that they thought back to was far more evocative than what happened to them in the lab. So, from that perspective, I don't think we're comparing like for like. If you asked me to imagine an angering or humorous situation from my past, I would come up with something really intense where I was truly furious or found a situation totally hilarious. Whatever I recalled would be more angering than not getting compensated for participating in research or more funny than "an individual releasing flatulence."

---

[5] To induce mirth in the moment, the researchers used a device called the "Wind Breaker", which does exactly what you think it does. But, so you have the joy of reading what I read, it is "a device consisting of a plastic container filled with a rubbery dough substance that when pushed down into the container produces a sound similar to that of an individual releasing flatulence."

[6] Yup, I have a mental list of favorite psychological studies about anger. That's the kind of nerd I am.

But that isn't really the point here. The point is that recollected stimuli (at least in the cases of humor and anger) can lead to a substantial increase in physiological activation. When you think about a thing that made you mad, you aren't just remembering a time you were mad, you're actually getting angry all over again.

Be Intentional with Your Memories

What should we do with the above information? Well, when it comes to the triggers we encounter each day that set off our emotions, we need to remember that they're not necessarily right in front of us. They aren't all things we encounter as we go through the world in our day-to day-lives. Sometimes an emotional trigger is a moment from our past that we might remember and therefore relive emotionally. That might be a good thing, if the emotion is joy, or it might be a bad thing, if it's an emotion you don't want to feel right now.

This plays out in our lives in all sorts of very real ways. We remember a funny moment from our past and burst out laughing. Or something triggers our grief as we're reminded of a loved one who passed away. These emotionally powerful memories might emerge at times we don't expect and have an impact on our current state of mind.

However, what this also means is that we can be more intentional about using these sorts of memories when we want to induce a feeling. We can activate our happiness by intentionally thinking back to positive moments from our past, and we can do that to counter a feeling that we no longer want to feel. Similarly, we should be aware of what it means to intentionally revisit angering or sad or scary moments from our past, because we could end up activating emotions that we don't want to activate in that moment.

Hack 8: Harness Your Imagination

Making Myself Mad

I was driving to work on a day when I was expecting a very contentious meeting. There was a particular person whom I expected to be hostile, and I started to run through all the different things they might say. In my head, I was preparing for the meeting, coming up with counterarguments and considering how I might phrase my rebuttals. While that may have been true – that I was preparing for the meeting – what I was actually doing was making myself angry in advance of any actual provocation.[7]

I bet this sounds familiar; maybe you've experienced it yourself with anger or some other emotion. You start anticipating bad news and get sad in advance. You imagine a scary thing that might happen in the future and you get scared as you think about it, activating that fight-or-flight response so your heart rate increases, your muscles tense up and you start to sweat, just as if something terrifying really is happening.

Actual vs. Recollected vs. Imagined

Let's take a moment to go back to the two studies I discussed in Hack 7. The researchers were inducing mirth or anger by asking people to remember something humorous or angering, or by asking them to imagine something humorous or angering, or they actually tried to activate humor or anger in the moment via a stimulus in the lab. In both studies,

[7] The punchline here, by the way, is that the meeting went fine. The person I was worried about didn't do any of the things I thought they might do and that anger I experienced on the way was all for nothing.

recollected emotion was more powerful than when the researchers used an actual stimulus right then and there.

What I left out of my previous account, though, was that *imagined* anger or mirth was as powerful as the recollected emotions. When participants were asked to imagine something humorous or angering, they experienced as much physiological activation as when they remembered something emotional from their past. In fact, even though the recollected and imagined emotions were both significantly more activating than the actual emotion experienced in the moment, they were not significantly different from each other. An imagined situation – something that had not happened – had just as intense an effect as a recollected situation.

The Power of Imagination

That's a really powerful finding about the strength of our imaginations and it offers a lot of possibilities for how we can hack our emotions. What it says more than anything else is that taking time to imagine something can give us an emotional boost ... or potentially take us down. For example, a socially anxious person who's invited to a party might get preoccupied with all the things that could go wrong and make themselves anxious in advance. Or, an insecure romantic partner might dwell on thoughts of their romantic partner breaking up with them, making themselves sad or scared without reason. We can make ourselves angry, sad, scared, guilty, etc. by imagining ourselves in a situation that evokes those emotions. We're likely unintentionally doing that on a regular basis – just as I did on that drive to work a few years ago, but it's also a skill we can use on purpose when we need to.

For example, in addition to using your imagination as an emotion hack to feel happier when you're down, you may also want to use it to put yourself in a particular mood. There are a host of professions, activities and other situations in which people perform best when feeling a certain way. For example, some athletes will say that they play better when they're angry and so they can visualize interactions that will make them mad before they perform.[8] You may want to feel more confident or secure before a job interview, so you take time to imagine yourself successfully navigating the interview. As a teacher or public speaker, I often find that I give a better lecture or talk when I'm feeling upbeat and positive, so I take steps to induce that state of mind in myself. Sometimes I'll watch a quick video online but other times I'll simply imagine something positive or funny happening. I might even imagine the talk going really well. Approaches like these, where you hack your emotions via your imagination, can set you up for emotional success.

[8] I sometimes do some humor writing for McSweeney's Internet Tendency. Humor writing is something I need to be in a particular mood for, feeling happy or even a little silly. I've found it helpful to learn to get myself into that mood instead of waiting for it to happen on its own.

CHAPTER 5
MOOD HACKS

It's a relatively simple and known truth that the mood you're in when you experience a trigger will influence how you respond. I'm certain you can think of a time when you reacted more intensely than you otherwise would have because you were tired, hungry or under a lot of stress. When we're in a relatively negative psychological or physical state, emotional triggers feel much worse and we react more intensely.

What follows from this logically is that we can be far more intentional about taking care of ourselves as a strategy for managing our emotions. Once you acknowledge that dehydration leads to increased emotionality, it's easy to see that staying hydrated can help prevent overreaction. When we understand that spending time in nature offers a sense of calmness that helps de-intensify negative emotions, it becomes clear that deliberately unplugging and taking regular walks outside will be beneficial.

In this chapter, we'll identify the variety of ways in which we can take better care of ourselves with the explicit goal of managing our emotions. As ever, I'll explore relevant research to help you learn to handle the triggers you'll inevitably experience if you prepare your mind and body through the following emotion hacks.

- Hack 9: Eat Well
- Hack 10: Prioritize Sleep
- Hack 11: Exercise Regularly
- Hack 12: Watch What You Drink

- Hack 13: Spend Time in Nature
- Hack 14: Manage Stress
- Hack 15: Engage with the Arts
- Hack 16: Recognize Your Mood in the Moment

In some ways, you can think of these different approaches as putting on a metaphorical seatbelt. By eating well, prioritizing sleep and staying hydrated, you're protecting yourself against those times when the road you're traveling gets rougher.

Hack 9: Eat Well

Hangry?

The first time I heard the term *hangry* (a portmanteau of hungry and angry) was in 2013[viii][1] when I read a HuffPost article titled "10 Things Hangry People Do".[ix] The word immediately resonated with me. I don't necessarily find myself getting hangry, but I do regularly see it in others, especially kids. But, of course, what I really wanted to know was what the research said about it. Is it real? Does hunger really lead to an increase in anger? If so, why?

Two years before this HuffPost article, a group of scientists published a research paper[x] to answer these questions, and they did so in an innovative way. Specifically, they were exploring the link between glucose levels and aggression through a series of four studies, with findings such as:

- participants who had consumed a glucose beverage behaved less aggressively than those who had a placebo beverage
- participants who scored higher on a test of diabetic symptoms had higher scores on tests of aggressiveness
- there's a positive correlation between state diabetes rates in the US and violent crime rates.[2]

---

[1]   Apparently this is 57 years after the first known use of "hangry", which was in a 1956 article on intentional wordplay in *American Imago*. This is according to a 2018 article on ABC News about how "hangry" had been included in the *Oxford English Dictionary* that year.

[2]   At least a few of you are livid right now, screaming "correlation is not causation" at the top of your lungs. I know, and so do the authors of that study. I don't think anyone is arguing that diabetes is a precursor to violent crime. This is just a single datapoint connecting blood sugar levels to aggression, and it supports what's been found in lots of other studies too.

A few years later, some of those same researchers did another study[xi] on a similar question, but this time they tracked married couples for 21 days, measuring their glucose levels twice a day. Every night before bed, those same couples would stick a voodoo doll, representing their spouse, with pins that reflected their anger levels. They found that low blood sugar predicted more intense anger.

Eat Your Way to a Better Mood

Of course, it's not just blood sugar that matters. There is plenty of research linking processed foods to stress and depression, and a relatively new body of research associates healthy gut bacteria with mood. In fact, nutritional psychiatry is an entire field that explores how food and nutrition can affect mental health, with the goal of preventing or even treating mental health conditions with dietary changes. Nutritional psychiatrists incorporate diet education and meal preparation into their treatment plans and they work with clients to help them better understand the link between what they eat and how they feel.

It's well beyond the scope of this book to cover nutritional psychiatry in any detail, but there are some relatively simple strategies you can embrace to impact your mood in a positive way. Here are some things you can do to shift your diet to improve your emotional wellbeing.

- **Limit processed foods and sugars:** These can lead to increased brain inflammation that is linked to depression and anxiety. Instead, try to focus on whole, nutrient-rich foods to maintain stable blood sugar levels.
- **Include lean proteins:** Chicken, turkey, beans, lentils and other lean proteins play an important role in building neurotransmitters such as serotonin and dopamine that regulate mood.

- **Eat the rainbow:**[3] Eating a variety of colorful fruits and vegetables ensures an intake of diverse vitamins, minerals and antioxidants that are important for emotional wellness. Such variety supports overall physical health and boosts mood by providing essential nutrients that enhance brain functioning.
- **Consume omega-3 fatty acids:** Found in foods such as fish and nuts, omega-3 fatty acids are known to reduce inflammation in the brain and support mood regulation. These healthy fats are important for improving communication between neurons.
- **Incorporate probiotics:** Fermented foods such as yogurt, kefir and sauerkraut promote a healthy gut microbiome, which is vital for serotonin production and overall mental health. This can improve mood, reduce anxiety and enhance emotional resilience.

There are obviously many reasons to eat healthily and emotional wellbeing is just one of them. It's worth noting that your diet impacts your emotional responses in a meaningful way and embracing good food choices will have a positive effect on both your physical and emotional health.

---

[3] As a person who sometimes struggles to remember all the different rules for healthy eating, this is my favorite piece of advice. I like that it's simple, clear and practical. I don't have to figure out how much of each food to eat. I just need to focus on healthy fruits and vegetables and embrace diversity.

Hack 10: Prioritize Sleep

Puzzle Trouble

I like to start my day with a cup of coffee and some short *New York Times* puzzles: Connections, Strands and the Mini Crossword. For me, it's a wonderful way to kick off the morning. It usually doesn't take too long and it feels good to get my brain going in a way that is low stress and low stakes.[4] I've noticed, though, a very direct relationship between a poor night's sleep and poor puzzle performance. I have a much harder time with puzzles when I haven't slept well, and I make far more mistakes. As importantly, they aren't as fun when I'm tired.

I've also noticed that my inability to think clearly when I'm tired is frustrating to me. I can sense myself not understanding things I should be able to understand and it makes me sad and irritated. There's a relatively direct link between my poor sleep and my mood; poor sleep leads to decreased cognitive ability, which in turn leads to decreased pleasure and satisfaction with the game.

The Cost of Fragmented Sleep

My experience with poor sleep has been borne out in some recent research, which finds that poor sleep can lead to difficulty regulating emotion. For example, most recently, a team of researchers[xii] explored a particular kind of disrupted sleep called fragmented sleep, which includes multiple awakenings or interruptions in a given night. It's different from sleep deprivation where you just don't get enough. In this case, you're in bed for enough hours, even asleep for

---

4   Don't tell my mom I said it was low stakes. She takes her *New York Times* puzzles VERY seriously.

most of them, but you keep waking up for brief periods that prevent you from feeling rested.

Here's what the researchers did and what they found. For 12 consecutive nights, participants had their sleep tracked via a wearable sleep monitor. On night five, they either had a control night or a fragmented sleep night. The control night was a regular night, but the fragmented sleep group was woken up every 80 minutes by an alarm that went off on their phone. In addition to the sleep monitoring, participants took a variety of emotion surveys and engaged in an emotion-regulation task where they watched some videos and were instructed to use some sort of regulation strategy.

What the researchers found was a little bit messy. The ability to regulate emotions wasn't directly affected by a lack of sleep but some skills were impacted. The next day, participants in the fragmented sleep group had a tendency to ruminate more (have repetitive thoughts that they couldn't seem to control), and that rumination led to some mood disturbances. Basically, poor sleep led to rumination and rumination led to emotional upset.

Part of what makes this sleep–emotion relationship complicated is that there's a bidirectional relationship at play here. Poor sleep leads to emotional disturbances and, in turn, those disturbances lead to poor sleep, and so on. In 2018, a review article came out that looked at much of the published research on sleep and mood,[xiii] finding that sleep deprivation led to more negative emotions and fewer positive ones. For example, the amygdala, the part of the brain responsible for initiating emotion, was found to be more active as a result of poor sleep, while the prefrontal cortex, the part of the brain controlling emotional impulses, was less active.

At the same time, this article found that emotion-regulation strategies, especially those rooted in cognitive-behavioral approaches, led to a better night's sleep. So, there are approaches we can use to set up a beneficial cycle of reciprocal causality (i.e., you can help improve your sleep by managing your emotions better, which will in turn make emotion regulation easier over time).

How to Sleep Better

Quite a few of the cognitive-behavioral approaches to emotion management will be discussed in Chapter 6, but I'm going to focus on sleep hygiene right now. Here are some strategies you can use to improve your sleep in a way that will improve your emotional wellbeing (which will likely improve your sleep further, and so on).

- **Maintain a consistent sleep schedule:** Try to go to bed and wake up at approximately the same time every day, even on weekends. This will help regulate your body's internal clock.
- **Create a relaxing bedtime routine:** Engage in calming activities such as reading, taking a warm bath or practicing meditation before bed as a way of signaling to your body that it's time to wind down.
- **Build a healthy sleep environment:** Do what you can to ensure your bedroom is cool, dark and quiet. A well-constructed sleep environment can prevent unwanted wake-ups that lead to fragmented sleep.
- **Limit exposure to screens before bed:** Try to decrease exposure to screens, including phones, tablets and computers, for at least an hour before bedtime. The light can interfere with your sleep schedule.
- **Limit naps during the day:** While short naps can be helpful, long naps can negatively affect your night-time sleep, especially when they are not part of a regular and consistent sleep schedule

- **Stay physically active:** Regular exercise can help you fall asleep faster[5] and enjoy deeper sleep. That said, try to avoid vigorous exercise close to bedtime as it can sometimes make it harder for you to go to sleep.

People often tell me that there's a vicious cycle that plays out here between sleep and emotionality. Bad sleep leads to negative emotions, which lead to bad sleep, and so on. They're right. The goal is to do the little things that help you sleep a little better, so you feel a little better the next day. Over time, those tiny changes will make a big difference.

[5]   And has a positive impact on your emotions, which is something we're going to touch on in Hack 11.

Hack 11: Exercise Regularly

A Nuanced and Complicated Relationship

In the introduction (*see* page 3), I shared with you that exercising *when angry* is unhealthy.[6] In fact, exercising in the middle of any intense emotion is typically unhealthy. I also wrote, though, that this relationship between exercise and emotion is nuanced and complicated and that we would discuss it more fully later in the book. I'm going to do that in two different places. Here I'm going to explain how physical fitness leads to emotional wellness. In Hack 44, I'll talk through why you should avoid vigorous exercise *when* you're emotional.

Central to this discussion is an understanding of how emotions are different from moods. Emotions are relatively short-lived experiences and are responses to some sort of trigger. Moods are longer-lasting patterns of emotions. So, sadness is an emotion, but if we feel it regularly for several weeks, we start to think of it as a mood state, and maybe even a diagnosable one (a depressive disorder).[7] This distinction is important because physical fitness is great for your mood and for your overall emotional health. It's just not great for dealing with immediate emotional arousal, because as I'll explain in Hack 44, it has the effect of elevating that arousal at a time when you probably want to decrease it.

---

[6] My explaining this fact on social media (and the responses I received after doing so) was actually the inspiration for this book.

[7] Depressive disorders are far more complicated than most people realize and it would be wrong to suggest that they are only long-standing patterns of sadness. For many people with a depressive disorder, it's not about sadness at all. It's about an absence of pleasure and joy. They don't report feeling sad necessarily, but they can't seem to find any joy in life.

A Better Quality of Life

In 2023, three psychiatrists from Jawaharlal Nehru Medical College in Wardha, India, did an exceedingly comprehensive review of the research on exercise and mental health.[xiv] They essentially reviewed every published study on this topic from the last decade to determine both the short-term and long-term benefits of exercise on emotional wellbeing. What they found was that regular physical activity had the following positive outcomes.

- **Enhanced mood** – decreased symptoms of depression and anxiety
- **Reduced stress** – decreased feelings of stress and reactivity to stressors
- **Improved self-esteem** – increased positive feelings about self, including body image
- **Improved cognitive functioning** – benefited cognitive functions such as attention, focus and memory
- **Improved sleep** – enhanced sleep quality, which we've already discussed (Hack 10) is associated with positive mood

The broad take-home from this article was that regular physical exercise reduces stress and improves mood and self-esteem, and can be "a valuable adjunctive treatment" for various mental health conditions.[8]

More specifically for our purposes, exercise improves your pre-stimulus mood, so you're in a more stable place when you do experience some sort of trigger. By decreasing stress, improving your overall mood, improving your sleep, etc., you're building a shield that protects you and helps you more readily endure losses, threats, provocations and other unpleasant stimuli.

---

[8]   The bit about being a "valuable adjunctive treatment" is really important. What psychiatrists are saying is that mental health providers should be prescribing exercise along with other treatments, something that does not seem to be happening regularly.

How to Get Active

While building a comprehensive exercise routine is beyond the scope of this book, here are a few recommendations to kick off an emotion-focused exercise plan.

- **Start by consulting with healthcare professionals:** Your general practitioner can help you determine if there are any existing health conditions you need to be careful of. They can also recommend an exercise specialist who can help you develop a realistic and healthy exercise plan.
- **Start small and gradual and choose activities you enjoy:** You should begin with modest goals in mind to help avoid injury and mitigate disappointment. Focus on activities you enjoy to help increase motivation and make exercising sustainable for you.
- **Focus on the mental health benefits more than on the physical ones:** The emotional benefits are pretty much immediate, so by concentrating on those, you're more likely to feel rewarded for your efforts. The physical benefits are going to come later, so people who focus only on those may get discouraged early on.
- **Vary your routine and build in social interactions:** Embracing variety will decrease boredom and keep the exercise sustainable. By building social interaction (e.g., joining a club, attending a class), you add another positive element to the workout and boost the psychological benefits.
- **Exercise outside:** As we'll talk about in Hack 13, just being in nature gives us psychological benefits. By exercising outside, you add another emotionally positive element to the experience.

To sum up, there are all sorts of benefits to healthy exercise and one of those is emotional wellness. Taking time to build a sustainable and fun exercise routine is a great way to protect yourself from unhealthy emotions.

Hack 12: Watch What You Drink

Water and Your Mood

In 2014, a team of eight researchers aimed to determine the effect of water intake on mood.[xv] They divided participants into two groups: "high-volume water drinkers" and "low-volume water drinkers"[9] (HVWDs vs. LVWDs) and instructed them to either decrease or increase their water intake. After a baseline period when the participants' fluid intake was monitored, there were three intervention days when the HVWDs had to reduce their water intake to 1 liter per day. The LVWDs had to increase their intake to 2.5 liters per day. Meanwhile, meals, sleep and other activities were standardized to minimize how much water was taken in through food or lost through sweat.

During both the baseline and intervention period, participants took several mood and other tests to monitor their emotional wellbeing. The intervention led to a considerable emotional shift for both groups. The HVWDs who decreased their water intake were less content, less calm, experienced fewer positive emotions and they had less energy. The LVWDs who increased their water consumption had more energy and fewer cognitive symptoms such as confusion.[10] Essentially, decreasing water intake made you moodier and increasing water intake made you less moody.

---

[9]   The term "high-volume water drinkers" is some next-level science jargon if all they're trying to say is that these participants drink a lot of water.

[10]   Not surprisingly, the group that decreased water intake was thirstier, and the group that increased water intake was less thirsty. So, there you have it: these scientists essentially proved that drinking water cures thirst.

Even Mild Dehydration Has an Impact

There are countless reasons to stay hydrated, including preventing unwanted anger, sadness and anxiety.[11] What this study essentially found – and it's consistent with prior research – is that even mild dehydration can significantly disrupt mood and cognitive performance, contributing to anxiety, depression and general irritability. Water is crucial for brain chemistry, helping transport oxygen and glucose. When we are dehydrated, these processes are hindered and our brain doesn't function optimally. We become more easily confused, forgetful and less able to concentrate.

These issues directly and indirectly impact our emotions. Forgetfulness, confusion and lack of concentration can be frustrating and anxiety-inducing. Also dehydration directly affects serotonin, a neurotransmitter involved in mood regulation. Without enough water, serotonin levels can drop, making us more prone to negative-feeling emotions.

Part of what makes this 2014 study so interesting is that we see how quickly the emotional impact of dehydration takes effect. A group of well-hydrated adults practiced low-water consumption for a relatively short amount of time (they were still drinking water, just not much water) and it immediately took a toll on their emotional health.

Be Cautious with Caffeine and Alcohol

Watching what we drink doesn't just include getting enough water. We also need to be careful about what we *do* drink because too much caffeine or alcohol can have a significant impact on how we experience and express emotions. For example, the short-term impacts for alcohol are obvious;

---

[11]   Also including, you know, sustaining life.

alcohol lowers inhibitions and impairs our judgment in ways that make us more emotionally reactive.[12]

In the long term, regular alcohol use is linked to higher rates of depression and anxiety. Over time, It has an emotional blunting effect where it dulls both positive-feeling and negative-feeling emotions. This blunting effect is rooted in the reason many people drink in the first place – as an attempt to numb some emotional discomfort (sometimes referred to as "self-medicating"). Neurologically, alcohol may disrupt some key emotion-relevant brain areas such as your prefrontal cortex (associated with impulse control) and your amygdala (the structure that initiates emotional responses). This disruption changes your capacity for emotional regulation, impacting both the experience and expression of your feelings.

Moderate caffeine use tends to have a more positive effect on our emotions, making us more alert and energetic. You become more focused, motivated and socially engaged. However, too much caffeine can make you irritable, restless and even anxious. Plus, it might lead to trouble sleeping, which you know from Hack 10 is associated with emotional dysregulation.

Takeaway? Drink Water

The primary takeaway here is relatively simple. If you already drink plenty of water, keep doing that and know that decreasing water intake will have a pretty immediate impact on your emotions. If you don't drink enough water,

---

[12]   This probably goes without saying, but other drugs have emotional consequences too. Nicotine can impact your stress response over time in a way that increases anxiety. In fact, nicotine addiction is rooted in part in the need for the drug to help regulate emotions. Meanwhile, long-term marijuana use can increase the risk of depression, impair emotional regulation and lead to apathy and emotional detachment.

you should start drinking more.[13] Similarly, be mindful of the consequences of alcohol and caffeine use (which also has the effective of dehydrating you), and recognize that there are long-term emotional impacts of consuming too much. Most importantly, pay attention to hydration as an intentional way to hack your emotions. Monitor your water intake and if you're feeling down, consider the possibility that you're dehydrated.

[13] In the introduction, I pointed out that being able to do many of the things in this book is a privilege not afforded to everyone. This is one example because adequate clean and safe drinking water is not available to everyone and yet dehydration takes a toll not just on physical health but on emotional health too.

Hack 13: Spend Time in Nature

"This is perfect"

When I was 16 years old, my dad and I were in New Mexico for a ski trip. He had a few work calls one morning, so we were going to get a later start than we expected. However, whatever he was meeting about turned into a big thing, and we got way behind. Eventually, he told me, "This is going to take all day. You should go without me." I was a little disappointed, but figured I would make the most of it.

It turned out to be one of the best days of my life. Nothing special happened. I didn't meet anyone. I didn't win the lottery. I just spent the day skiing on my own, which I had never done before. Because I was on my own, I enjoyed the natural beauty of the mountains in ways I never had before. This was an era before cellphones, and as I had no one to talk with, I just spent the day looking around. I love the mountains. I always have. And even though I had always made a point of taking in the views, I had never done it quite like I did that day. It was a beautiful day and I spent it alternating between skiing and pausing to look around and enjoy the scenery. Not only the mountains but the trees, the snow, the sky. I was happy that day in ways I hadn't really experienced before. I remember thinking at one point, "This is perfect."

Mental Health Benefits of Being in Nature

There's a long history of research on the psychological benefits of spending time in nature. In 2021, a paper[xvi] came out that reviewed the previous decade of research into the impact of nature exposure on overall health. Across the studies reviewed, the researchers found significant emotional and mental health benefits from time spent in nature. It reduces stress, leads to more positive emotions and improves cognitive functioning.

For example, in a 2015 study,[xvii] researchers randomly assigned participants to one of two groups. There was a Nature Walk Group, who would walk for 50 minutes through a natural environment, and an Urban Walk Group, who would walk along a heavily trafficked road. Both groups took a variety of surveys (e.g., Positive and Negative Affect Schedule, The State-Trait Anxiety Inventory, and others) before and after the walk. What the researchers found was really extraordinary. After just 50 minutes, the Nature Walk Group, as compared to the Urban Walk Group, experienced lower levels of anxiety, increases in positive mood, a decrease in rumination and improvements in working memory.

What makes this study particularly interesting is that it controls for exercise. The Urban Walk Group was still getting the physical experiences of a walk, so the mental health benefits of exercise – the ones I outlined in Hack 11 – were available to both groups. Because of that control, we can surmise that the benefits gained by the Nature Walk Group really had to do with exposure to the natural environment.

The theory behind this is rooted in the work of Drs. Rachel and Stephen Kaplan, two environmental psychologists who wrote the book *The Experience of Nature: A Psychological Perspective*[xviii] back in 1989. In it, they articulated how urban environments are more cognitively demanding than natural ones because you have to filter out a number of distractions (e.g., traffic noise), and dealing with those demands leads to fatigue. According to the authors, being in natural places restores the cognitive resources that are depleted from spending time in more complicated urban environments.[14]

---

[14]   This is actually called "Attentional Restoration Theory (ART)," which is going to get confusing later when I discuss the emotional benefits of exposure to actual art (Hack 48).

As Simple as Just Getting Outside

In a lot of ways, spending time in nature really is as simple as just getting outside, but here are a few ideas for things you can do to improve your mood through nature.

- **Take regular, short walks in nature:** Brief forays outside throughout your day can offer relatively immediate benefits, especially if you've been engaging in cognitively complicated tasks. Find a nearby green space to go for a walk.
- **Unplug:** Do what you can to disconnect from technology while you're in nature. If you're looking at your phone, reading emails or texting, you won't get the same benefits as if you set your technology aside.
- **Engage mindfully:** Related to unplugging, be intentional about focusing on your surroundings by getting out of your head and looking around with awareness. In fact, a 2024 study found that birdwatching on a nature walk led to better emotional outcomes than just going on the walk, presumably because looking for birds required the person to focus on nature.[xix]
- **Seek environments that gently grab your attention:** Try to find natural settings that encourage you to pay attention to them – what is referred to as "soft fascination." Gently moving water, the wind in the trees and the sounds of birds all encourage you to notice them in a way that doesn't feel cognitively demanding.
- **Use all your senses:** To the degree that you can, try to engage with nature through as many senses as possible. Paying attention to what you can hear, smell and feel,[15] instead of just see, can be really helpful and healthy.

---

[15]   You probably shouldn't taste the nature ... unless you've got some expertise around foraging.

The benefits of spending time in nature are extensive. Engaging mindfully and intentionally with the natural world can go a long way in replenishing our emotional stores and preventing discomfort and exhaustion.

Hack 14: Manage Stress

Yes, But It's Complicated

There's a question I've been asked over and over again in the last three years. I've heard it in almost every interview I've done since 2020 and it's on the minds of pretty much everyone I talk to when they find out I study emotion. Are we angrier now than we used to be?

I suspect the answer to that question is yes, but it's complicated. It's a hard question to answer because there's no real way to track that sort of thing. We don't have some international anger thermometer that monitors how mad people are. The best we can do is to estimate based on other factors such as the number of road-rage incidents or reports from service providers. Both of those indicators, by the way, would tell you that, yes, there is more anger now than there used to be.[16]

So my final answer is that I don't know for sure, but I think we are in fact angrier than we used to be, and I suspect that one of the reasons is because stress is so pervasive for so many people right now. For the last five years, we have been dealing with considerable worldwide political unrest and conflict, an international health crisis, natural disasters and economic uncertainty. These very real stressors have put strain on people in ways that make them more likely to get angry ... not to mention sad and scared.

---

[16] This is a wildly incomplete assessment, though, because anger can be expressed in so many different ways. Add to that the fact that historically and currently there have been marginalized groups who have experienced incredible injustices and are rightfully angry. Many of those groups didn't have a safe opportunity to express that anger in the past, so it may have existed then but been invisible to many people in ways that it is no longer.

Amplifying the Negative Feeling

If you think in terms of the Why We Feel Model we've been using (see page 14), this stress we're experiencing impacts our mood at the time of the stimulus. If I'm already tense and I encounter an unexpected barrier or a loss, that existing tension amplifies the negative feeling. I get angrier or sadder than I otherwise would have done. That happens largely because that tension shifts the way we interpret or appraise the stimulus. We think of the stimulus as "just one more thing" on top of a bunch of other stressors and it feels even worse.

For example, imagine you're under a lot of pressure in your personal life. You've had some unexpected family health concerns and you're worried about your finances. It's been a lot for you, and you haven't been able to manage it very well psychologically. You then go to work where things have been going relatively well comparatively. However, you learn that one of your co-workers hasn't completed their part of a project and now you're behind. On its own, it's not a crisis. It's just a delay. But coupled with the other stressors you've been experiencing, it feels overwhelming. Work had been a place for you to escape some of those other problems, but now it's a source of additional worry.

This relatively minor problem feels like a major problem, and you start to spiral with a host of negative and catastrophic thoughts. It begins to feel like the world is caving in on you. What if you lose your job? Will that mean no money and no health insurance? Now that work is threatening to go badly, your other problems seem infinitely worse.

Obviously, we can't control everything that happens to us and we're all likely to experience stress in our lives. Bad things will happen to us and they will cause us stress, so we need to identify ways of dealing with and managing that stress.

Taking Care of Yourself in a Holistic Way

Many of the hacks I've mapped out so far in this book are also ways of managing stress. Eating right, staying rested, exercising, spending time in nature, etc., are all healthy and productive stress-reduction methods. And many of the upcoming hacks will also be good approaches to dealing with stress (the same reappraisal strategies given in Chapter 6 to manage emotions will also work for managing stress). However, here are a few additional approaches you might find helpful when feeling overwhelmed by external stressors.

- **Regular deep breathing**: Taking regular breaks in your day to breathe deeply can help you bring down your arousal levels, making you less likely to overreact when faced by a provocation (we'll discuss deep breathing in Hack 40).
- **Setting boundaries:** Saying no to optional requests that aren't consistent with your goals or don't sound fulfilling can be a valuable way of protecting your time and decreasing stress.
- **Cultivating gratitude:** Writing down things you are thankful for can help you shift your focus away from stress to more positive thoughts.
- **Planning, prioritizing and delegating:** Taking time to plan and prioritize, breaking tasks up into manageable steps, can help make life more manageable. Asking for help or delegating work when appropriate can also be a mechanism for protecting your time.
- **Connecting with others socially:** Spending quality time with your friends or loved ones or joining a community of people with similar interests can also help shift focus away from stressors.

The central thesis of this part of the book is that if we take care of ourselves in a holistic way by eating right, sleeping well, staying hydrated and engaging in other healthy habits, we'll respond more positively when we experience negative situations. Managing our stress is an important part of that.

Hack 15: Engage with the Arts

"Can I audition for this?"

When one of my sons was nine years old, we went to see the musical *Finding Neverland* at a nearby performing arts center. He had seen plenty of shows before and had always enjoyed them, but this one seemed to hit him differently. My son was completely enthralled, rapt in the production, leaning forward in his seat and taking in every moment. I felt like I needed to remind him to breathe, he was so totally and completely into it. I don't know exactly why this one felt different to him, but I suspect it was because there were so many kids in it. He could imagine himself performing in ways he hadn't before. As we walked out, he asked, "When I'm double-digits years old, can I audition for this?"

To me, this is but a tiny example of what engaging in the arts can do for our emotional wellbeing. It helps us feel connected to others, distracts us from our problems, inspires us and brings us joy. This sort of engagement can be defined broadly, from watching a concert to visiting an art gallery to attending a poetry reading. It also includes creative self-expression through performing, drawing, painting, writing, taking a ceramics class or any one of a myriad of other activities. Engaging with the arts can look a lot of different ways and we have good reason to believe all those ways are valuable for your emotional health.

To be clear, I'm not saying that you need to channel your emotions into creativity for it to be valuable. We'll talk about that specifically in Hack 48. The point I'm making here is that engaging in the arts by attending workshops, concerts, plays, art shows and so on helps prevent negative emotions from taking hold. Much like exercise, hydration and healthy eating, engaging in the arts offers a buffer against fear, sadness, anger and loneliness.

More Valuable than Physical Health or Employment?

There's a relatively new body of research around the positive impact of creative pursuits on your state of mind, with two research studies in particular showing its value. In 2024, a study published in *Frontiers in Public Health*[xx] used the results of a national survey of 7,000 people across England to explore the relationship between arts and crafts and emotional wellbeing. The researchers found that participation in crafting activities such as painting, sculpting, knitting, woodcarving and pottery led to improvements in life satisfaction, happiness and feeling as though life is worthwhile. Unlike other research, this study didn't see a reduction in loneliness, but that's probably because so many of these activities are done alone (there's no need to engage socially when knitting or drawing the way there might be if you attend a concert). Maybe the most impressive finding here is that participating in arts and crafts was as valuable or even more valuable than physical health or employment in the prediction of happiness and life satisfaction.

Even more interesting is a 2022 study from *Frontiers in Psychology*[xxi] that looked at 44 studies from the previous seven years exploring the impact of community-based arts activities on emotional and social wellbeing. What's fascinating here is that the researchers were intentional about not including research from therapeutic settings. They wanted to know about the impact of projects that involved direct interaction with the community, such as music workshops, public art projects or dance classes. The researchers found that arts engagement led to improved self-esteem and decreased loneliness.[17] They also found that these benefits were more

---

[17] Unlike the arts and crafts survey previously mentioned, this study includes projects that require people to engage with others – so there's a social component that likely explains the decreases in loneliness.

substantial for marginalized groups such as people of color or the elderly. Finally, they found that active participation (e.g., creating art or performing) had a greater impact than just observing.

How to Engage with the Arts

True confession here: I'm not a very good artist. I end up consuming far more art than I create for that reason. To be honest, I've let not being very good at it steal some of the benefits. It's hard to enjoy drawing or making ceramics when you are so often disappointed with the outcome. Therefore, for me, the first tip below – find an activity you enjoy – was particularly important.[18]

- **Find an activity you enjoy and engage regularly:** There are so many arts to choose from, so take time to try new things and find something fulfilling. Then, do that activity regularly to fully see the benefits.
- **Build the activity into your daily life:** Try dedicating a few minutes each day to your creative activity, using it as a break from work or stressors. Small and consistent efforts can enhance happiness and life satisfaction.
- **Prioritize active participation:** While there are emotional benefits to observing artistic endeavors such as performances or concerts, the best results come from engaging in an active way. Prioritize those activities where you are creating rather than just viewing or listening.
- **Take the opportunity to connect with others:** Even if your particular art form is typically done in solitude, find ways to engage with a community around that art by taking classes, joining clubs or taking part in collaborative projects.

---

[18]   That activity is humor writing for me, and it's what I try to carve out time for whenever I start to feel overwhelmed and challenged by my job.

- **Use the activity as a tool for reflection:** One of the benefits of engaging in a creative activity is that it can provide an outlet for self-expression and personal growth. Be intentional about using the activity to help you process emotions or gain new perspectives.

Whatever your level of skill, nurturing creativity in your life has a transformative potential, enhancing feelings of self-esteem, contentment and happiness, and boosting your emotional wellbeing. What's more, the more you practice your chosen artwork, the more skillful and proud of your achievements you will become.

Hack 16: Recognize Your Mood in the Moment

"How's the weather down there?"

In 1983, two researchers, Drs. Norbert Schwarz and Gerald Clore, did a study on life satisfaction.[xxii] It was a telephone survey where they called people up and asked them, "How satisfied or dissatisfied are you with your life as a whole these days?" Participants answered on a scale of 1 to 10, with 10 being most satisfied.

However, the researchers' goal wasn't actually to assess life satisfaction. They were exploring something much more intriguing. They knew the locations of the people they were calling and they were keeping track of the weather at those locations, so they were looking for relationships between weather and life satisfaction. The researchers found that, indeed, people reported a lower level of life satisfaction on rainy days compared to sunny days.

Let's take a moment to unpack this finding because I think it's more interesting than it might appear at first sight. We know that weather influences mood, but that's not what the researchers found here. What they found was that weather influenced a person's reported satisfaction with their life *as a whole*. People thought their life, overall, was worse on rainy days than on sunny days. Logically, that doesn't make much sense. Your overall life doesn't change much based on the weather on a particular day.

Yet what does change is your mood. What seems to be going on here is that the weather was influencing their mood – so they felt down if it was raining – and feeling down caused them to rate their overall life more negatively. This alone is interesting, but what's even more fascinating is what happened next.

In a follow up, the authors decided to draw attention to the weather by saying, "By the way, how's the weather down there?" as part of the interview. When they did this, forcing people to pay attention to the weather and indirectly their mood, the differences went away. People no longer rated their life worse on rainy days. By paying attention to the negative thing that was influencing their mood, their negative evaluation of their life was improved.[19]

Catch Your Emotions

Here's why paying attention to our emotional state is so important. There are a lot of little things that influence our emotions on a given day (e.g., the weather, stress, hunger, temperature). These things often operate unnoticed. For example, we may feel physically uncomfortable because it's too hot in our office, and that influences our emotions in a way that we don't realize. We snap at people, not because the person did anything significantly wrong but because we're feeling out of sorts and whatever they did ends up seeming worse.

What if taking a moment to acknowledge the physical discomfort we're feeling can help us better manage our emotions? What if we do the equivalent of asking, "How's the weather down there" and simply take stock of our psychological and physical states more regularly? Can saying to ourselves, "Right now, I'm feeling [sad, angry, scared, hungry, tired, uncomfortable, stressed]" help us respond more positively when we're confronted with a negative experience?

---

[19] Another example of this is to pay attention to your actual physical surroundings. Look at the room you're in right now as you read this. Is it tidy or is it messy? Is it too cold or is too warm? Are the lights too bright? Not bright enough? These seemingly little things might be influencing your emotions in ways you don't realize, but by paying attention to them, you might undo their impact.

I know we've discussed something similar in Hack 3, Log Your Moods, but this is a little different. With Hack 3, we were talking about collecting emotional data over time and then using that data to make decisions about how to influence your emotional patterns. Here, the hack is about learning to catch the emotions as they're happening to you.

How Am I Feeling Right Now?

I have two suggestions for you here. First, start being intentional about regularly assessing your emotional and physical status. Ask yourself frequently how you're feeling (defined broadly) in a given moment. Pay attention to things such as hunger, stress, sadness, anxiety, fatigue and other states that could be and probably are influencing your emotions. You can do this by regularly asking yourself, "How am I feeling right now?"

My second suggestion is to take this a step further by asking what impact that state might be having on your emotional reactivity. For example, if you identify that you're anxious or tired, ask yourself how that might be making your emotional reactions more intense. Might you be responding more negatively to a trigger because you're fatigued? Might your anxiety be causing you to feel far worse about a relatively minor problem? Taking stock of our emotional, psychological and physiological states might offer us a mechanism with which to hack our emotions in the moment.

CHAPTER 6
INTERPRETATION HACKS

Arguably, the most important predictor of when and how you'll emote is your interpretation of the stimulus you're experiencing. This is the root of many therapies for emotion-related problems such as depression or anxiety. When you get sad, it's because you interpreted the stimulus as a loss. You appraised the thing that happened as negative or even hopeless. When you get scared, it's because you interpreted the stimulus as a threat. You decided the thing that happened is dangerous. Your interpretation may be correct, by the way. These things may legitimately be hopeless or dangerous. Regardless, your emotional response is rooted in the interpretation and not the actual stimulus.

Of course, what follows from this argument is that shifting that appraisal would change the emotional response. Even if it doesn't change the emotional response entirely (i.e., even if you don't shift from sadness to happiness), it can change the intensity of how you feel. Moving, for example, from a thought of "This is the worst thing that could have happened" to "This is really frustrating" will help decrease the anger you feel in that moment.

Psychologists have identified a number of different thought types that can either exacerbate or alleviate negative emotions. In this chapter, I'll describe some of these thought types that, through subtle changes, can be shifted in a way that leads to healthier emotions. You'll learn to identify common problematic thoughts through the following hacks.

- Hack 17: Unpack Your Worldview
- Hack 18: Drop the Labels
- Hack 19: Avoid Catastrophizing
- Hack 20: Refocus on Planning
- Hack 21: Avoid Overgeneralizing
- Hack 22: Avoid Misplacing Blame
- Hack 23: Identify Your Core Beliefs
- Hack 24: Check the Entitlement
- Hack 25: Deal Effectively with Rumination
- Hack 26: Challenge Self-Directed Shoulds
- Hack 27: Embrace Positive Reappraisal
- Hack 28: Use Acceptance Appropriately
- Hack 29: Put Things into Perspective
- Hack 30: Refocus on the Positive
- Hack 31: Don't Make It About You
- Hack 32: Don't Expect Changed Behavior
- Hack 33: Avoid Considering Opinions as Facts
- Hack 34: Don't Dismiss Positives

The key here is not to lie to yourself. If something really is terrible, it's healthy to describe it as terrible. The goal in this chapter is to learn how to embrace realistic thoughts that accurately describe the circumstances in which you find yourself.

Hack 17: Unpack Your Worldview

"I can't believe that guy"

I was out one night bowling with friends. When it was time to leave, we went to pay and my friend gave the guy working there a $20 bill to pay for two rounds of bowling. The guy gave my friend change as though he'd only given him $10. My friend said, "I gave you a twenty," and the guy said, "My bad," and gave him another $10 in change. That was the entire interaction.

We left the bowling alley and went to a nearby bar to grab a couple of drinks. Twenty or so minutes later my friend said, "I can't believe that guy tried to screw me."

"What are you talking about?" I asked, legitimately confused.

"The guy at the bowling alley tried to steal my change," he said.

I was really surprised by his reaction. This had struck me as a simple mistake that was easily addressed and had no real consequences. In contrast, my friend understood it as an intentional attempt to steal from him. We saw the exact same interaction play out, but walked away with wildly different interpretations. The tough part about this for me, though, is that I can't honestly say that I know my interpretation is the correct one. I think it is, but I'm sure my friend thought his was the correct one too.

What I am sure about is that our interpretations probably had very little to do with the actual interaction and a lot more to do with our individual worldviews. I suspect what was really going on was that my friend tended to approach the world with a certain amount of mistrust and that mistrust impacted how he interpreted situations like these.

Worldviews and Schemas

A worldview is a comprehensive, overarching framework of how the world operates. It includes our values, assumptions, biases, beliefs and expectations of the future. You can think of it as a broad, big picture understanding of the world. Your worldview often operates as a lens through which you take in information. For example, a person may have a religious worldview that includes the existence of an interventionist God. Many experiences they have will be filtered through that worldview's lens; they are thankful to God when they get good news or they ask God for strength when they experience challenges.

A related concept, a schema is a mental framework for a specific thing (e.g., a situation) and it's often based on past experiences or information you've learned. You can think of a schema as this helpful mental shortcut that allows us to navigate and understand situations. If your friend tells you she's going on a date one evening, you don't have to ask her to explain what a date is because you've got a mental representation of it. If she tells you it's a first date, that mental representation may shift slightly because you have a different schema for a first date.

In developing treatments for emotion-related problems, Dr. Aaron Beck – who most people consider the founder of cognitive therapy for emotional disorders – described something called the "cognitive triad,"[xxiii] which is a set of schemas people have about themselves, the world (i.e., other people) and the future. You might view yourself as lazy and unimportant. You might view others as cruel and untrusting. You might view the future as bleak. You then interpret information and experiences through these lenses. When you have a success, you write it off as an unimpressive accomplishment that anyone could have done (because you're seeing it through the lens of you being lazy and unimportant). You view that success as inconsequential in the long run because you see the future as grim and hopeless.

When my friend got the wrong change at the bowling alley, our different interpretations were likely the result of us having different schema for the world. I tend to be a relatively trusting person who views other people as having good intentions but capable of making mistakes. He tends to view other people as untrustworthy and wanting to take advantage. For me, the incorrect change was a simple mistake that was easily corrected. For him, the incorrect change was an intentional act to steal from him.[1]

Unpacking Your Worldview

To fully manage your emotions in a healthy way, you have to do something really difficult, and that's to understand your own worldview and schemas. You have to think about how you view yourself, others and the future (along with a host of other schemas you may have) and how all that might inform your emotional reactions to situations.[2] Spend time considering the assumptions you make, the biases that affect your feelings and your expectations for the future. Here are a few strategies you might use.

- **Journaling:** Take time to write about your thoughts, feelings and reactions to daily events, with a focus on the belief system that might have led to them. You can use some prompts like, "What assumptions did I make when that happened?"

1   I actually wish I knew which one of us was correct. Maybe this guy really was trying to take advantage of my friend and I missed it because my schema of others having good intentions clouded my vision and judgment.

2   One of the challenges here is that the people with the most problematic worldviews often have the hardest time understanding or shifting them.

- **Self-questioning:** Challenge yourself by asking tough questions and even arguing with yourself. Asking yourself, "What evidence do I have for this?", "Is there an alternative explanation?" or even "How might someone else view this situation?" can help you better understand your schemas.
- **Engaging with others openly:** One way to uncover your schemas is by interacting with people with different perspectives. By reading books, seeing movies, listening to podcasts or just having conversations with people who think differently than you, you'll start to understand more about both their worldview and yours.

Most importantly, when you ask yourself the above questions, do so nonjudgmentally. The goal isn't to decide if your worldview is accurate (though you may come to see things differently through this process). The goal is to better understand that worldview and how it informs your feelings.

Hack 18: Drop the Labels

Five Types of Angry Thoughts

More than 20 years ago, my advisor, Dr. Eric Dahlen, and I developed a paper-and-pencil test called the Angry Cognitions Scale that was designed to measure five types of angry thoughts. It consists of nine one-sentence situations you might experience in your day-to-day life along with the types of thoughts you might have in those situations. For example, if you were driving through a residential neighborhood and someone backed into the street and almost hit you, would you think something like this?

- "Nobody knows how to drive any more," or
- "That dumb jerk," or
- "They must not have seen me."

By providing these sorts of scenarios, we were able to identify some of the common thoughts people have that lead to anger. We were also able to pinpoint some important differences between people with anger problems and people without anger problems.

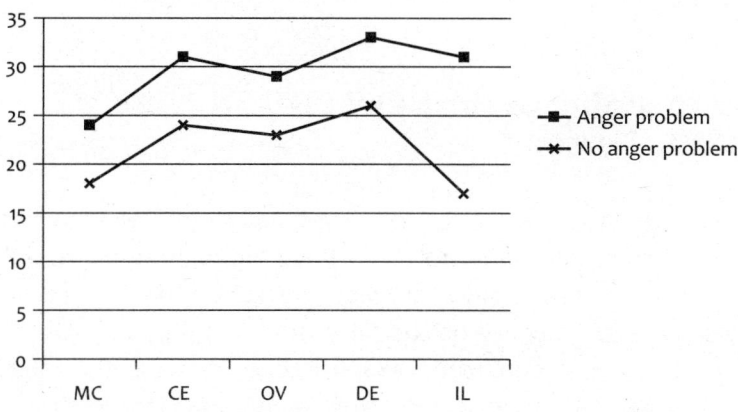

In the chart, the top line represents people for whom anger has been a problem. They get angry more often than others and experience more regular anger consequences. The bottom line represents people who don't have anger problems. They get angry less often than most people and rarely, if ever, experience anger consequences. Both lines indicate their scores on the five types of thoughts measured by the scale:

- Misattributing causation (MC)
- Catastrophizing (CE)
- Overgeneralizing (OV)
- Demandingness (DE)
- Inflammatory labeling (IL)

We're going to talk about all five types at various points, but for now, let's focus on the last one. Pay attention to the gaps between the two lines for each of those thought types. For four of them, the difference between angry people and calm people is between 5 and 8 points. That's significant, but not nearly as great as the difference in that last thought type, inflammatory labeling, which is about 15 points. What this indicates is that the biggest difference between angry people and calm people is the tendency of the former to label others in a negative or inflammatory way.

Responding to the Label instead of the Person

Once you label someone – once you call them "an idiot" or "a monster" or "manipulative" – you stop responding to the person themselves and start responding to the label you've given them. They are no longer a human being, capable of nuanced and complicated motivations. They are the label you've given them. In reality, people are complicated. Smart people are capable of doing dumb things. Kind people are capable of doing cruel things, and honest people are capable of lying. We lose sight of that when we label them in a specific way.[3]

This is especially true when we don't know the person very well or at all. For example, you're driving somewhere and another driver cuts you off badly. You don't know this person. They're just a stranger on the road. You can call them an "idiot" or a "hazard",[4] and because you have nothing else to go on, it's easy for that label to stick. Even though they obviously did something hazardous, saying "That was dangerous" is healthier than "That person is a danger."

Seeking Accurate Definitions

The lesson here isn't that you should never define anyone. It is that you should try to define people accurately given the information you have. You should also recognize the limits of the information you have and acknowledge those gaps. Most importantly, you should hang on to the idea that people are able and likely to do things that are inconsistent with that label.

Here are some ways to address a tendency to label.

- **Notice it when it happens:** Pay attention to the language you're using and notice when you define people in a singular way, especially when it's inflammatory

---

[3]   You can see clearly here how the labels you use are probably rooted in your worldview (discussed in Hack 17). A person who is fundamentally untrusting of others is going to be more likely to label someone a "liar" or a "cheat."

[4]   I know full well that you would probably call them something far worse. I'm just trying to keep it clean.

- **Reframe labels to focus on actions instead of identity:** Instead of saying, "They're a fool," say, "They did something foolish."
- **Practice empathy:** Try to see the entire person you're dealing with in a given situation and understand that they are complex beings capable of both good and bad acts.

What we haven't yet acknowledged here is that we don't just label other people. We label ourselves too. We call ourselves "idiots" or "stupid" or "lazy", and those labels have a similar impact on our emotions. When we label ourselves as disorganized or unmotivated, we start to respond to ourselves only in terms of those labels and we ignore the times we have operated outside them. We get down on ourselves in the same way we might get down on someone else we perceive as disorganized or unmotivated.

Once again, the solution shouldn't be to lie to ourselves. If we behave foolishly or selfishly, it's OK to call that out. The pathway to self-improvement starts with an honest assessment of our deficits. The goal is to be honest with ourselves in a nuanced way. Saying, "I wasn't very organized around this task" is different from saying, "I'm not an organized person." We need to pay attention to those differences and embrace missteps as possible opportunities for growth.

Hack 19: Avoid Catastrophizing

First and Second Takes

During the interpretation stage of emoting, we evaluate two things: (1) the stimulus and (2) our ability to cope with the stimulus. For example, in Hack 18 when we talked about labeling, that was an example of us evaluating the stimulus. The "primary appraisal" is our first take on a situation, when we make quick decisions about what's going on and who is responsible. Many of the emotion hacks we're going to discuss in Chapter 6 will be about better understanding how we're engaging with this initial response (the primary appraisal).

With this hack, though, I want to highlight the second part of our appraisal process, your second take on a situation. This is what psychologists call the "secondary appraisal", when we evaluate our ability to cope with the stimulus. For example, imagine you get some bad news at work: one of your team has taken another job and will be leaving in two weeks. They are a very good employee and you become consumed with anxiety about how you'll be able to replace them. You start saying things like:

- "We'll never be able to function without them."
- "I'll never be able to replace them."
- "This place will be awful without them."

In moments like these, whether what you're telling yourself is true or not, what you're doing is catastrophizing. You're evaluating the stimulus – the person's announcement of their departure from work – in a highly negative way and deciding that you can't cope with it.

Interpreting the Situation

Catastrophizing has significant emotional consequences because it intensifies negative-feeling emotions. Taking the example above, imagine two alternative interpretations of this same event (a team member getting a new job).

1. This is an absolute disaster. We're right in the middle of this project and there's no way I'm going to be able to get it all done without them. Plus, work just won't be any fun if they're leaving. Why did this have to happen?!
2. I always knew they might get another better job, and even though this is disappointing, I should be happy that they're moving on to a great role. I've got two weeks with them still here, so I better use that time to transition their work to other employees and come up with a replacement plan.

Notice that the second interpretation doesn't include emotional denial. You aren't pretending everything is OK. You are acknowledging the disappointment and the very real challenges ahead. But you're also taking a problem-solving approach to mitigate the long-term difficulties. In fact, it's through the honest acknowledgment of disappointment that you're able to shift your attention to solutions. If you were denying the reality of the situation, you wouldn't attend to the need for practical actions.

In this example, we're talking about fear and disappointment but any emotions can be affected by catastrophizing. Your guilt after an error is intensified when you catch yourself saying, "I'll never be able to bounce back from such a stupid mistake." Your anger when wronged is much stronger if you say, "This is the worst thing they ever could have done." When we catastrophize, we exacerbate the negative feelings of whatever emotion we're experiencing.

Try to See Things as They Are

So, how do you minimize catastrophizing without slipping into denial? One of the best ways is to do an honest and realistic assessment of the consequences you're facing. What are the actual outcomes of this situation? What will it really mean in the context of your life? You can do this when faced with relatively small and simple triggers (e.g., when you forget something at home and have to go back for it, ask yourself how many minutes you'll be delayed and what the real consequences will be of that lost time) or with much more significant situations such as the loss of a job or the ending of a relationship. By evaluating the real consequences while also avoiding exaggerated negativity, you allow your emotions to be much more realistic and healthy.

It can also be empowering to acknowledge and embrace the true outcomes when faced with a challenging situation. By shifting away from catastrophizing and focusing on a realistic understanding of what is happening, you set yourself up to problem solve in a way that will be helpful moving forward. Once you understand the true scope of a situation, you can work toward fixing it.

Hack 20: Refocus on Planning

You Can Choose Your Thoughts

So far in Chapter 6, I've been focusing on thoughts to avoid (e.g., stop catastrophizing, stop labeling). Discontinuing those types of thoughts is important because engaging in them keeps you immersed in the negative emotions. However, at the same time it's helpful to intentionally shift to more positive thoughts. In other words, it's easier to stop catastrophizing if you have something else to do with your mind. That's one of the benefits of refocusing on planning.

The goal is to shift your attention away from negative thoughts or distressing emotions and instead focus on actionable steps that will move you in an emotionally healthier direction. For example, imagine your partner passes away. It's a truly and legitimately terrible loss that brings with it a host of emotional and practical consequences. Along with the intense grief – sadness, anger, fear, hopelessness and other complicated feelings – there are likely very real concerns about the future. You may now have unexpected financial problems, childcare challenges and big questions about what your future looks like. It's understandable to catastrophize in a situation like that, thinking of all the terrible things that have already happened and the other awful things that could go wrong. In doing so, you add additional anxiety and hopelessness to the pain you're already experiencing.

Refocusing on planning is when you shift away from those catastrophic thoughts and start planning out strategies to deal with whatever bad thing has happened. In this case, maybe you go meet with a financial planner to talk through your financial concerns. Or perhaps you go to a family member or friend to talk through your childcare issues and ask for some guidance or assistance in solving them. This sort of planning does two things for you emotionally: (1) it takes you out of your negative thinking in a way that decreases at least some of the anxiety, and (2) the planning empowers you by giving you more emotional confidence moving forward.

How to Refocus on Planning

Here is a four-step process that will help you replace your negative thoughts with more useful and practical ones. Like any good cognitive emotion-management strategy, it starts with identifying the unhelpful or dysfunctional thoughts.

1. **Identify the unhelpful thought.** For example, imagine you have an extraordinary amount of work to get done for your job. At first, you're focused on the work and you think, "I'll never get all of this done" or "I'll never catch up." Though natural, these thoughts are relatively unhelpful and anxiety-inducing. Identifying them in the moment is a really important first step because it gives you a point to intervene.

2. **Label the actual feeling.** The next step is to take a moment to acknowledge the emotions; in this case, anxiety. Too often, people try to ignore or minimize the actual feeling by saying things to themselves like, "It's fine" or "It's OK" or even "It is what it is." Those things might ultimately be true, but it's healthier and more honest to tell yourself something like, "I'm feeling really anxious right now because of all the work I have." Emotions, positive or negative, impact us whether we acknowledge them or not, so labeling the feeling is a healthy way to proceed that allows you to adjust strategically.

3. **Build out a plan.** Once you understand the problem and the emotion – in this case, too much work and the anxiety that follows that – it's time to build a plan that will allow you to accomplish that work. As a college professor, I would regularly find myself with an overwhelming amount

of grading to do. My "refocus on planning" approach in those moments was to make a realistic schedule for getting it all done and then to follow that schedule as closely as possible. A key word here is *realistic*. Creating an unrealistic plan in these moments might end up harming you even more because of the emotional impact of falling behind. If I map out a grading plan that can't reasonably be accomplished, that anxiety won't just return but might return more intensely. In addition to renewed catastrophizing, I might also turn to some self-disparaging thoughts about my failure to meet my goals ("I couldn't even get this done. Why can't I just focus?"). By setting more conservative and realistic goals, I will save myself a lot of potential negativity.

4. **Act on the plan.** Once you've mapped out how you are going to deal with the problem you're facing, you need to implement whatever solutions you've generated. In the grading example, I would probably start easy with something like, "I'm going to grade five papers in the next hour and then give myself a break." By acting on that and staying focused, I start to feel less anxiety because I've replaced the catastrophic thoughts with proactive thoughts. And I also start to feel empowered because I'm taking reasonable steps to solve my problems in a realistic way.

Hack 21: Avoid Overgeneralizing

Never vs. Rarely

Imagine you send a text to a friend with a specific question. Maybe it's even a time-sensitive question so you're hoping for a quick response. After a few minutes without them replying, you think to yourself, "People never text me back right away."

There's a specific word in that thought that might be causing you problems and that word is "never." When you use words such as "never" or "always" or "every" or "nobody," you're likely engaging in a specific form of problematic thinking called overgeneralizing. This is when we use overly broad language to describe situations or people. You hear it a lot when people talk about frustrating experiences. This kind of thinking matters because when you say something *always* happens to you, your emotional response isn't just about the one moment – it's about a whole imagined pattern.

This is going to sound a little nitpicky, but there's a big difference between "never" and "rarely." There's also a big difference between "always" and "usually." And those differences matter. Much like the discussion of labeling earlier (Hack 18), the words you use influence how you think of situations, so when you say, "People *never* text me back," you're responding to a different provocation than the one you're actually experiencing. What's happening to you is you're waiting on a single time-sensitive response from a particular person.[5] It may be frustrating, but by saying "People never text me back," you've made it something else entirely. It's no longer about a single person not texting you

---

[5] There's another conversation we can have about whether or not it's reasonable to have such expectations. You wanting a quick response doesn't necessarily mean that someone can/should/is obligated to provide you with one (*see* Hack 24). Managing our expectations of ourselves and others is an important emotion-regulation tool.

back as quickly as you wanted but about how people, more generally, never text you back. So now, emotionally, you're responding to a much bigger problem than the one you're really facing.

It's also probably untrue. Some people will sometimes write you back right away. Even if you have some friends who sometimes respond slower than you would like, you've probably had plenty of instances when people responded as quickly as you wanted them to. So, you've not just turned an individual situation into a pattern, you've also created an inaccurate perception of a pattern.

Overgeneralizing Makes a Difference

When people really pay attention to their thoughts, they often catch themselves using overly broad language. They see their co-worker check their phone while they're speaking, and think, "No one ever listens to me." Their children leave a light on and they say, "They never remember to shut off the lights." They're given the wrong food in a fast-food restaurant and they think, "They do this every time."

The difference between "always" and "sometimes" might seem like a small one, but it's not. Research shows that people who regularly overgeneralize tend to experience more negative emotions.[xxiv] You may remember from Hack 18, Drop the Labels, that overgeneralizing was one of the five types of thoughts measured by the Angry Cognitions Scale, and that's because this thought type is particularly relevant to anger. When you turn other people's single behaviors into a pattern of behavior, you are more likely to get angry.

But overgeneralizing doesn't just lead to anger. When it rains and you respond with, "Ugh, it rains every day here," you're more inclined to get sad about the weather. When you're about to do a presentation for school or at work, and you think, "I always mess these up," you're more likely to get anxious.

Healthy Ways to Shift Your Thinking

The good news is that it's possible to shift your thinking in moments when you're prone to overgeneralize. Here are some strategies for moving away from overgeneralizing.

- **Assess the accuracy:** When you catch yourself using "always" or "never," pause and ask whether those words are really true. Does your friend truly *never* initiate plans, or just not as often as you'd like? If the pattern is real and problematic, your frustration may be justified – but it's still helpful to describe it accurately.
- **Intentionally use precise language:** Try to replace overgeneralized wording with something more specific. Shifting from "My boss always ignores my ideas" to "My boss has dismissed my last couple of suggestions" can help you feel less trapped by a distorted pattern of thinking.
- **Don't dismiss real patterns:** Your tendency to overgeneralize doesn't mean patterns don't exist. If your romantic partner regularly arrives late for things, it's reasonable to acknowledge that as a problematic pattern. If a colleague often takes credit for your ideas, it's valid to acknowledge that issue. The key is to recognize the pattern accurately, rather than exaggerating it in a way that fuels unnecessary negativity.

Recognition and Practice

In dealing with all the different thought patterns above, there are two critical activities: (1) recognition and (2) practice. These strategies are only going to work if you can recognize when you're engaging in an unhealthy thought pattern. That sort of self-understanding takes time and practice because people often don't realize in the moment what they're doing.[6] Learning to catch yourself requires a willingness to pay close attention to the thoughts you have, to reflect after the fact and to admit when you've made a mistake. None of those things are easy to do, but intentionally practicing them is part of the journey to a healthier emotional life.

[6]   I was recently talking to a friend about their tendency to overgeneralize when I caught myself saying, "You always do that. You always blow things out of proportion." While I'm not terribly proud, at least I caught it and corrected myself.

Hack 22: Avoid Misplacing Blame

It's Not Always What You Think

If there's one thing that psychologists are really good at, it's taking basic terminology and making it sound way more complicated than it has to be. This is what we've done with "misattributing causation," which is basically just a fancy way of describing a tendency to place blame incorrectly.

Misattributing causation takes a few different forms. First, sometimes we blame the wrong person entirely. Imagine you come home from a stressful day at work and see muddy footprints tracked across the kitchen floor. Immediately, frustration bubbles up as you assume one of your kids walked in without taking off their shoes.[7] Later, you realize the real culprit was your spouse who was on a work call at the time and planned on coming back to clean it up afterwards.

However, other times we blame the right person but for the wrong reasons. Say you're waiting on a friend to meet you for dinner, and they show up 20 minutes late. You feel hurt and assume they must not value your time or that they're just inconsiderate. You spend those 20 minutes feeling down and annoyed. But when they get there, they explain that they were stuck in unexpected traffic. The delay still causes frustration, and maybe some disappointment that you don't get as much time together, but misattributing the cause led to some unnecessarily negative feelings along the way.

People who frequently misplace blame tend to assume the worst possible explanation for someone's actions. If a colleague forgets to invite them to a meeting, they assume it was deliberate rather than an oversight. If their partner is short with them, they assume it's because they're annoyed with them rather than stressed about work. This kind of

---

[7]   Maybe you mix in some overgeneralizing here by saying, "They always do this."

thinking fuels unnecessary tension, leading to greater frustration, sadness and even anxiety.

Don't Jump to Conclusions

Like labeling (see Hack 18), catastrophizing (see Hack 19) and overgeneralizing (see Hack 21), misattributing causation is one of the thought types measured by the Angry Cognitions Scale (see Hack 18). That research, along with later work using that scale, shows that this tendency to jump to conclusions can have significant emotional and social costs. Studies suggest that people who misattribute causation are more likely to experience heightened stress, engage in unnecessary conflict and hold grudges longer than those who take a more balanced approach to interpreting situations.[xxv]

Relationships, romantic and otherwise, can also suffer when we assume bad intentions where none exist. The example above with the friend who arrived late demonstrates just this. Imagine if the late friend hadn't offered an explanation or if the waiting friend hadn't inquired about the lateness. The incorrect interpretations might have lingered in a way that eroded their friendship. Communication is important, obviously, but so is making a point of not jumping to potentially unhealthy and inaccurate conclusions.

Breaking the Blame Habit

It takes time and effort to stop misattributing causation, but there are some practical steps you can take.

- **Consider multiple explanations:** When faced with an upsetting circumstance, pause and consider the most likely explanation. Try to avoid jumping to conclusions or assuming the worst. For example, before assuming that someone ignored your text on purpose, consider other possibilities – maybe they were busy, maybe they forgot, maybe their phone died.

- **Be intentional about gathering more information:** There will be many times when you don't exactly know what's going on, so make sure you understand the situation fully before you emote. If you find mud all over the floor, take a breath before assuming who left it. It's possible that your initial reaction was correct, but it's better to be sure.
- **Examine your own role:** It's easy to blame external factors, but sometimes negative emotions stem from our own actions (or we're at least partially responsible). For example, when my students do poorly on an exam, I can externalize that blame completely ... or I can acknowledge that I might not have taught them well enough. The reason for the poor performance is probably a little bit of both.[8]

Misattributing causation is a common thinking error, but by recognizing it and working to correct it, we can reduce unnecessary emotional distress and improve our relationships. Learning to question our first reactions helps us build a more rational, compassionate and emotionally balanced way of seeing the world.

---

[8] I get a surprising amount of pushback on this concept. Someone inevitably says, "But if some of your students do well, you can't be the problem." This is probably false. In every class, there are students who do well despite their teacher. It would be naïve and arrogant for me to think I'm responsible for my students' success but not responsible for their struggles.

Hack 23: Identify Your Core Beliefs

Convictions Drive Your Emotions

Around 2015, I was running an all-day relay race with some friends. It had been a long but really fun day. When the race was over and we were all leaving, I couldn't find my car keys. I hadn't used them since I parked the car early in the morning and I assumed they were in my workout bag, which was very full, but I just couldn't find them. It would be normal to be a little anxious in a situation like this, but I really overreacted emotionally. I could feel myself panicking as I thought about all the ways this would be a problem. Would someone have to come pick me up? Would my friends have to drive out of their way to get me back home? After a few minutes of searching, I ended up finding them, but the anxiety over what was ultimately such a small thing lingered.

With Hack 17, I discussed the need to better understand your worldview, describing it as "a comprehensive, overarching framework of how the world operates." Your worldview includes your values, assumptions, biases and expectations. It also includes your core beliefs: those deeply held convictions about yourself and the world around you. These core beliefs are critical to your emotional wellbeing because the feelings you have in any given moment are often rooted in them.

For example, let's say that one of your core beliefs is that your worth is defined by your success at work. That belief will inform your emotions relating to your job. When you struggle professionally, it will feel far worse. When you're successful, it will feel far better. Those struggles and successes are tied to this deeply held belief, so when you don't get a promotion, the sense of failure is intensified and so is the sadness that follows. When you receive praise from a supervisor, the sense of success is similarly intensified and so is the joy that follows.

Other examples of core beliefs might be "Everyone else's happiness is more important than my own," "I must always be in control" or "Other people's love is conditional." Beliefs such as these, which are some of the building blocks of your broader worldview, drive emotional responses in relatively predictable ways. They may lead you to sacrifice your own happiness for others, react with greater anxiety when things feel out of control or feel insecure in relationships.

"It's terrible to be a burden"

One of my core beliefs is that it is terrible for me to be a burden to others. I don't like asking favors of people and I don't like being in situations where people have to do things for me. I get anxious if I feel like I am in the way, and it's particularly uncomfortable for me if I feel as if I've made a mistake that complicates other peoples' lives.

This core belief is what drove that race-day anxiety. I was panicking because I could feel myself becoming a burden to my friends. Even as I searched through my bag, I felt like I was holding them up. They didn't want to leave until they knew I had found the keys, so they were waiting, and I hated that I was making them wait. In my mind, they were all tired and just wanted to get home, and I was preventing that. And what if I couldn't find the keys? That would mean one of them would have to drive me home and that would feel even worse.

I now recognize this core belief of mine and I am very intentional about noticing when it is informing my emotions. If I'm delaying other people in some way, I check in with myself to see how much anxiety it might be causing. I ask myself how responsible I am for the delay or if this is just bad luck. I also ask myself how upset I would be if the situation were reversed and other people were delaying me. The fact that I understand this about myself allows me to navigate those situations that would be otherwise anxiety-provoking for me.

Identifying Your Core Beliefs

Here are three steps to take to identify your deeply held convictions, starting with paying attention to moments when you had strong – maybe even overly strong – emotional responses. Like the lost keys example above, those moments may be useful in revealing some of your fundamental beliefs.

1. **Pay attention to common triggers:** Think about those moments when you've had strong emotional responses (e.g., anger, sadness, fear, shame or even intense joy). Identify the broad types of situations where you tend to have big emotional reactions.
2. **Then, look for patterns:** Try to identify what those situations have in common. Are there themes running through them all, such as feeling rejected, criticized, unappreciated or something else? What are the common elements that connect these types of situation that leave you feeling emotionally overwhelmed?
3. **Now, ask what these patterns mean:** At this point, you want to dig a little deeper to question what these reactions tell you about yourself. For example, if you identify a pattern of feeling rejected, perhaps your core belief is that people will abandon you or that you are not important to other people.

Identifying these core beliefs provides you with important insight that will be helpful when you experience strong emotions in the future. Being able to tell yourself, "I'm reacting strongly right now because [I'm scared of being abandoned, I'm scared of being silenced, I don't believe people care about me]" is an important step in managing your own emotional responses.

Hack 24: Check the Entitlement

Just Because You Want It

Another thought type (*see* Hack 18) that is associated with negative emotions, especially anger and frustration, is demandingness. Just like it sounds, demandingness is when you believe your own needs, preferences or expectations are more important than those of others. When people hold on to this belief, they don't just want things to be a certain way, they *demand* it, often reacting with anger or frustration when the reality doesn't align with their expectations.

For example, imagine you're at a coffee shop in the morning, and the barista is moving a little slower than you'd like. You might think, "They should be moving faster – I've got to get going!" In that moment, you've placed your schedule above the challenges they might be facing, whether it's being short-staffed, dealing with a large order or simply needing an extra moment to do their job well. You also may be putting your wants above the wants of other customers who may have similar time constraints or who may be ahead of you in line.

Of course, a related concept is entitlement, whereby we believe that we are deserving of special treatment, privileges or benefits, regardless of whether we actually did anything to earn them. It's the assumption that positive outcomes should come our way not because of effort or merit, but just because we want them.

Again, imagine that after a date, a man becomes frustrated when the other person declines a second meeting. Instead of accepting their decision, he insists that because he paid and treated them well, the other person should give him another chance. His belief that kindness or financial gestures guarantee romantic interest is rooted in entitlement and fuels his anger.

Inconvenient or Intolerable?

In some cases, demandingness and entitlement can escalate into a sense of injustice. If you're in a restaurant waiting for your food, mild impatience might turn into outright fury. You might be thinking, "This place should have enough staff to serve me immediately!" Instead of recognizing a minor inconvenience, we frame the situation as something unfair or even intolerable.

Like the other thought patterns I've talked about, demandingness is strongly linked to anger issues. Research shows that people who think this way tend to get angrier more frequently and react in ways that create problems for themselves and others. Such people are more likely to seek revenge, lash out or experience negative consequences from their anger.

And it's not just anger. Thoughts of demandingness and entitlement lead to other negative emotions such as sadness or jealousy. When a person doesn't get something they were expecting, they don't just get angry, they feel sad or even hopeless. When a student doesn't get into a college they believe they should have gotten into, instead of simply feeling the understandable disappointment, they feel a deep sense of unfairness too. Similarly, when someone gets a promotion you believe you were entitled to, it leads to jealousy and resentment ("I've worked here longer. It's me that should have been promoted.").

Managing Demandingness and Entitlement

So, how can you manage these feelings? Here are some strategies.

- **Question your expectations:** When you start feeling sad, angry or jealous because you didn't get something you wanted, pause and ask yourself, "Are my expectations reasonable?" Step back and assess whether you're actually being treated unfairly or if you're merely frustrated that things aren't going your way. You can even take this a step further and ask yourself why you believe you deserve this (that may connect back to a core belief).

- **Acknowledge real unfairness:** This isn't about ignoring injustice – sometimes, people really are treated unfairly. If that's the case, it makes sense to be upset. The key is distinguishing between legitimate injustice and you just not getting something you really wanted.

- **Be on the lookout for other negative thought patterns:** Demandingness often becomes more problematic when it's paired with thoughts such as catastrophizing ("This is the worst thing ever!") or overgeneralizing ("This always happens!"). If you don't get something you want and you believe it's going to lead to a catastrophic outcome, it's obviously going to feel far worse. Try to recognize and challenge those patterns as well.

- **Practice gratitude instead of comparison:** Sometimes demandingness stems from a tendency to focus on the things you don't have. Instead of focusing on what you believe you *should* have, focus on what you *do* have. Gratitude can reduce entitlement by shifting your mindset away from what's lacking to what's already present in your life.

The more you let go of demandingness, the less frustration, anger and sadness you'll experience in everyday situations.

Hack 25: Deal Effectively with Rumination

Can My Son Read Minds?

I was driving home from my eldest son's school one day when he was about six years old. He was sitting in the backseat listening to music and I was thinking about my day. I don't know what, specifically, I was thinking about, but I know it must have been dramatic and I was on a bit of a rant in my mind. I was having these racing thoughts about something that had happened that day, thinking through the interaction, what I'd said and what I wished I'd said, when I heard my son say, "What did you say, Dad?"

"Nothing, buddy. I didn't say anything," I responded, thinking he must have heard something else and thought it was me.

"Yeah, you did," he said and then repeated my entire last thought to me, verbatim. I was left with one of two possibilities. Either my son could read minds ... or I was saying my thoughts out loud without even realizing it.[9]

Though not always (or even usually) spoken out loud, this is an example of rumination,[10] or the experience of continuing to think about the same thoughts, typically negative or distressing ones, in a repetitive and unhealthy way. We may replay recent events (which is what I regularly do) or we may have a series of obsessive thoughts about the future.

[9] My students have confirmed that it's the latter. One student, Sammy, used to have a desk outside my office and would regularly shout to me, "You're talking to yourself again!"

[10] It is a little bit ridiculous for me to write a chapter about how to deal effectively with rumination when I've been so very bad at dealing with it myself. That said, the entire point of this book is that you don't need to be great at all 50 of the hacks. You just need to be able to do some of them well, do some of them kind of well, be willing to work at others and ignore the ones that don't seem like a good fit. This is one where I've still got some work to do.

These rumination episodes are typically not solution focused, though. They are often just a replay of a situation, and what happens is that they keep the person trapped in a cycle of negative emotions.

Your Brain's Default Mode

Neurologically, what's happening here is connected to what's called the default mode network (DMN), a set of structures in the brain associated with rest (i.e., the parts of the brain that kick in when you're not focused on external tasks). When you're doing something that requires attention (e.g., writing, driving, talking to a friend, the dishes, etc.), you're using what's referred to as the task positive network. This is the parts of your brain that are active when you're attending to something. But when you stop doing those things – when your brain no longer has to focus on a task – your mind gets to wander. You start daydreaming, thinking about past events, etc. This is your DMN at work. It's the parts of your brain that kick in when you're not focused on a specific task. For some people, the mind wanders off to something great (a trip you want to take, a book you just read). But for some of us, it wanders off to some negative emotional experience.

A 2023 study[xxvi] explored the role of the DMN in rumination by comparing two groups: (1) highly emotional (i.e., neurotic) participants and (2) emotionally stable participants. Both group's brains were scanned via functional magnetic resonance imagining (fMRI) while they listened to either critical comments (e.g., "You can be very self-involved at times") or praising ones (e.g., "I like your sense of humor"). What they found was that criticism activated the DMN in highly emotional people – those with a tendency to experience negative emotions such as anxiety, sadness and anger – significantly more than praise did. Essentially, what happened is that these critical comments activated the rumination centers of the brain, but only in people who were prone to emotionality.

What this study tells us more than anything is that difficult-to-control rumination is associated with negative emotions and seems to be caused, in part, by activation of the DMN. As importantly, this study reveals some possible interventions for unhealthy rumination.

Disrupting the DMN

As emotional problems and rumination are linked to DMN activity, interventions should focus on disrupting that ruminative process. Another way of saying this is that if moments of "rest" lead to ruminative mind wandering, you need to find ways to direct your restful thoughts toward something else. Here are some ways to do that.

1. **Meditation:** Try shifting your focus away from your ruminative thoughts and onto the present moment. Practiced regularly, meditation strengthens your ability to control your wandering mind.
2. **Body scanning:** Similarly, when you bring attention to your physical sensations via a body scan, you are less absorbed in negative thoughts, breaking the cycle of rumination.
3. **Socializing:** Engaging with others helps redirect your focus away from ruminative thoughts and toward those external conversations.
4. **Expressive writing:** You can externalize your worries by writing about your thoughts and emotions. This can also bring clarity to your thoughts and feelings and help reduce emotional intensity.
5. **Structured problem solving:** Embracing more intentional problem solving will help you move away from passively dwelling on problems. Find solutions by breaking big problems down into more manageable steps.

Ultimately, the goal here is to shift your focus away from the negative emotion loop you've found yourself in. Each of the above tips does this in a different way. By disrupting the DMN, you activate more positive and proactive thinking that will decrease the negative thinking.

Hack 26: Challenge Self-Directed Shoulds

The Greatest Culprit

I've been collecting data via The Anger Project[xxvii] for about four years. It's a simple survey that asks people how often they get angry, why they get angry and what sorts of consequences they experience as a result. It also asks who they tend to get angry with. And this is where I learned what I consider to be the project's most interesting finding.

While people do indeed get angry with their co-workers, their family and their friends, the single greatest culprit is ... themselves. Approximately 75 per cent of participants say that they are likely to get angry at themselves. The only other group that was close was family, at 72 per cent. After that, it was politicians and other drivers at 58 per cent and 55 per cent, respectively.

The survey itself doesn't ask any follow-up questions so I took to social media to ask my followers what they thought. What I learned was really fascinating. Over and over again, they said things like, "I get mad at myself when I don't accomplish my goals" or "I get mad when I say I'm going to do something and then can't get myself to do it." Essentially, almost all of that self-directed anger could be explained by one specific type of thoughts: self-directed shoulds.

Internalized Expectations

Self-directed shoulds are your internalized expectations of yourself.[11] They are the demands you place on yourself; the

---

[11] Dr. Albert Ellis, founder of Rational Emotive Behavior Therapy, famously told people to "Stop shoulding on themselves." Though to me, that just sounds like another *should*. Oh really, Albert, *should* I stop shoulding on myself?

things you think you must accomplish in order to consider yourself successful, worthy and good enough. These types of shoulds aren't all bad. They can motivate personal growth and prosocial behaviors such as giving and volunteering. When you tell yourself, "I should stay in good shape" or "I should be kind," you're using self-directed shoulds that encourage a variety of positive behaviors (e.g., exercise, healthy eating, giving).

At the same time, self-directed shoulds can have a negative impact on your emotional life when your standards are too high or otherwise unrealistic. Or, perhaps the standards aren't necessarily unrealistic, but you are too hard on yourself for failing to meet those standards. For example, imagine that one of your shoulds is that you should *always* be productive or you're wasting time. When you violate this should to spend time relaxing with a friend, you find yourself feeling anxious that you'll fall behind in your work, angry at yourself for taking a break or even sad that you can't seem to enjoy your downtime.

Or maybe the self-directed should encourages you to do things that aren't in your best interest at a given time. If one of your shoulds is that you want to be there to help others, you might so overextend yourself that you experience stress or anxiety. In this case, it's not that you're failing to meet your own expectations. It's that you're meeting them in a way that is damaging to you. You help your co-worker or classmate on a project and the consequence is that your own work suffers.

You can see how these self-directed shoulds are often connected directly to your belief systems, which is one of the reasons it's so important to unpack your worldview (Hack 17) and identify your core beliefs (Hack 23). For example, one of my core beliefs is that it feels terrible to be a burden to others, which translates into self-directed shoulds such as "I should be independent," "I should not make anyone wait for me" or "I should not ask for help." In many ways, these self-directed shoulds are your core beliefs translating into the thoughts you have about yourself in a given moment.

Redirecting those Shoulds

How do you handle your self-directed should, alongside with identifying and challenging your core beliefs? Here are some strategies.

- **Reframe your shoulds as *coulds*:** If you start to think of your self-directed shoulds as preferences, the overall tone and resulting feelings change. Instead of saying, "I should always be productive," try shifting it to, "I'd like to be productive." Instead of saying, "I should never be a burden to others," try shifting it to, "I would like to be independent, but sometimes I'll need help."
- **Evaluate the origin story of the should:** Take some time to think about where the should came from. Where did you learn it? Is this something your parents taught you? Or something you learned from society more broadly? As part of that evaluation, you can ask yourself if it's still serving you in a healthy way or if it's something you could let go.
- **Look for evidence:** Sometimes it's helpful to try to identify some evidence to support your self-directed should. For example, if you tell yourself that you should always be productive, ask yourself if you know anyone else who is *always* productive. You might look for evidence, too, of how important rest is to achieving your goals.
- **Practice self-compassion:** Finally, when you catch yourself engaging in self-directed shoulds, try to respond with some kindness. Give yourself some grace by silencing that inner critic with positive self-statements. I know this may sound a little cheesy, but it's worth asking if you would ever talk to other people the way you talk to yourself.

I want to reiterate that there's nothing wrong with having high standards for yourself. In fact, failing to have high enough standards can also be a problem. It's when those standards are unrealistic that the emotional challenges tend to reveal themselves.

Hack 27: Embrace Positive Reappraisal

Shifting from Disappointment to Solutions

I'm going to tread carefully with this one because if there's one thing people don't want to hear when they are feeling down, it's something akin to "look on the bright side." It's a little bit like telling an angry person to relax or calm down. It barely works, if ever.

There's a test I've used quite a bit in my research called the Cognitive Emotion Regulation Questionnaire (CERQ).[xxviii] It measures nine types of thoughts people have when they've experienced a negative life event. Many of those thoughts (e.g., self-blame, rumination, refocus on planning) we've already discussed and a few (e.g., acceptance, putting into perspective) we'll discuss later, in Hacks 28 and 29. Right now, I want to focus on positive reappraisal, which is the cognitive skill of reframing a stressful or negative situation in a more positive way. It's when you think things like, "I can learn from this," or "What can this teach me?" in response to a disappointment.

My 13-year-old son is a basketball player. He loves it. It's by far his favorite activity. This last year, his school decided to have two teams, a gold and a silver team. They held a tryout and to his (and my) surprise, instead of being picked for the gold team, he was listed as floating between the two teams, playing sometimes with gold and other times with silver. At first, this shook him in a significant way. He wasn't expecting it and it really rocked his confidence. Over the next week, though, I watched him shift his thinking to one of opportunity. He started talking about how playing with silver team would give him the chance to develop his leadership skills. He acknowledged that he might not have the best attitude on the court and this might have been holding him back. Mostly, he shifted to what he'd learned from the disappointment and how he needed to work harder and practice more.[12]

Looking for the Positives

My son's case is an example of how positive reappraisal can work in real life.[13] When we lose a job, we can be disappointed while also recognizing that there's an opportunity to explore new career paths, learn new skills and find a job that's a better fit. When a relationship ends, we can be sad while simultaneously recognizing how the relationship helped us grow and how it will help us build healthier relationships in the future. When an appointment is unexpectedly cancelled or rescheduled, we can get frustrated yet also embrace the extra time to listen to a podcast or music or just reflect on our day.

The research shows that positive reappraisal works too. In 2005, I did a study with Dr. Eric Dahlen where we used the CERQ, which measures positive reappraisal along with those other eight thought types, to explore the relationships between positive reappraisal and sadness, fear, anger and stress. [xxix] We found that there was an inverse relationship between the use of positive reappraisal and all four of these states (sadness, fear, anger and stress). When people were intentional about looking for positives or thought about how they could become stronger as a result of what had happened to them, they were less likely to feel sad, scared, angry or stressed.

---

[12]   Some potentially positive self-directed shoulds in action.

[13]   I remain confident that this only worked because neither my son's mother nor I told him to look on the bright side. He came to these conclusions mostly on his own with us guiding him and supporting him instead of telling him how to think or feel.

Learning to Positively Reappraise

We know positive reappraisal works, but we also know it's difficult and that it's especially hard to coach people on it in the moment (i.e., people tend to respond badly when told to consider the positives). So, with that in mind, here are some ways to embrace this sort of positive reappraisal when it suits you and when it's appropriate.

1. **Be patient with yourself:** For many people, practicing positive reappraisal requires unlearning some habitual negative thought patterns that they may have spent decades learning. Make sure you recognize that this will be a gradual process with setbacks and you need to be patient with yourself.

2. **Be intentional about positive reframing:** It is completely understandable that your first reaction to a disappointment will be some sort of negative thought (catastrophizing, blaming, etc.). But once you've worked through some of that initial sadness, grief, disappointment, anger or fear, take some time to be intentional about a positive reframe. Ask yourself questions such as, "What can I learn from this?" or "Are there any new opportunities here?"

3. **Adopt a growth mindset:** At its core, positive reframing is borne out of a belief that personal development rises from adversity. Try to build a worldview whereby you see challenges as opportunities for learning and growth. That sort of worldview will help to reinforce the habit of positive reframing.

4. **Surround yourself with positive influences:** It's difficult to engage in positive thinking when you're surrounded by negative people. Engaging with people who regularly practice positive reappraisal or other sorts of positive thinking will shape how you learn to interpret difficult situations.

As with other thought patterns, the goal here isn't to lie to yourself. You're not trying to reframe a negative experience into a positive one at the expense of the truth. This isn't about minimizing the negative impact of the situation. The things that happen to us can and often do have both positive and negative outcomes. At its best, positive reframing is about acknowledging the negatives as real disappointments while also looking for the positives.

Hack 28: Use Acceptance Appropriately

A Nuanced Approach

Of all the thought types, positive and negative, described in this book, none is more complicated and nuanced than acceptance. This is the process of acknowledging reality as it is, including a recognition of life circumstances and the emotions that come with them.

What makes acceptance complicated? Well, if you go back to that 2005 study I described in Hack 27, Dr. Eric Dahlen and I, and also the authors of the Cognitive Emotion Regulation Questionnaire (CERQ), found that it was the only thought type not to behave the way the original authors of the scale expected it to. They (and we) expected some thoughts (e.g., self-blame, rumination) to be related to negative emotions and some other thoughts (e.g., positive reappraisal, acceptance) to be inversely related to those negative emotions. What we found, though, was that acceptance was moderately (instead of inversely) correlated with sadness, anger, fear and stress. This means that those participants who embraced acceptance were more likely to feel those negative emotions.

There's a good reason for this finding, and it's relatively simple: acceptance isn't practiced in just one way, yet the CERQ seems to measure a particular type of acceptance. Consider these items from the CERQ, which participants are supposed to agree or disagree with, for example:

- I have to accept that this has happened.
- I cannot change anything about it.
- I must learn to live with it.
- There is nothing I can do to change it.

These aren't necessarily empowering thoughts. Telling yourself, "I cannot change anything about it" sounds an awful lot like hopelessness. Even if there is nothing you can change, that's not the sort of thought that will lead to positive emotions.

Active vs. Passive Acceptance

There are different forms of acceptance and they have different impacts on our emotions. For example, active acceptance is associated with a realistic understanding of a situation, including what can and can't be changed about it. When you actively accept something, you're acknowledging that reality, while also making decisions that will improve your emotions within that situation.

Passive acceptance, on the other hand, means resigning yourself to a situation. You're accepting the situation as impossible to change and you're not embracing any active coping strategies. Telling yourself, "I must learn to live with it" is far more passive than saying, "I'm going to accept this but find a way to grow from it." The first approach is likely to lead to hopelessness and sadness while the second is empowering and hopeful.

In addition to these forms of acceptance, you'll find psychologists also talk about radical acceptance (a full accepting of reality as it is, very similar to active acceptance), self-acceptance (accepting yourself, including your strengths and weaknesses without excessive criticism) or even situational acceptance (accepting your circumstances fully and completely, similar to self-acceptance). How you might choose to employ these different forms of acceptance matters to your emotional wellbeing – hence the nuance.

Finding Healthy Acceptance

As a general rule, embracing a more active form of acceptance is far healthier for your emotional wellbeing than passive acceptance. For example, take losing a job. Passive acceptance would include removing any personal agency from being able to find a new job or learn from the experience ("This is terrible and I'll probably never find as good a job again"). Yet active acceptance would include acknowledging that reality, including how disappointed you are, but also identifying where you have control and agency ("This is terrible, but I'm going to focus on what's next for me"). With all that in mind, here are a few ways to achieve the emotional benefits of acceptance.

1. **Prioritize active rather than passive acceptance:** As you know, passive acceptance leads to resignation and helplessness, while active acceptance allows you to acknowledge reality and take meaningful steps forward. By choosing active acceptance, you shift from feeling powerless to focusing on constructive ways to move on productively.

2. **Identify what you can and can't control:** A critical step in embracing a more active form of acceptance is learning to distinguish between what is within your control and what is not. This helps you direct your energy toward productive actions rather than frustration. Understanding what you can and can't change in a situation is a skill that requires effort and practice.

3. **Reframe acceptance as a strength and not a weakness:** It's really important to understand that acceptance is not about giving up. It's about having the strength and courage to face reality and respond practically rather than resisting what can't be changed. Embracing acceptance as a strength allows you to move forward with clarity, resilience and self-empowerment.

Ultimately, despite the complications, acceptance is a powerful tool for resilience, allowing people to acknowledge reality while focusing on what they can control. Much more than passive resignation, true acceptance is an active process that fosters growth and meaningful forward progress.

Hack 29: Put Things into Perspective

Of Course, It Could Be Worse

Very high on the list of things you don't want to say to a person while they're emoting intensely is, "It could be worse." Much like telling a person to "Look on the bright side" as a way of encouraging positive reappraisal, it comes across as minimizing and insensitive.[14] Ultimately, the problem is that of course it could be worse. That's always true. You could be dealing with everything you're dealing with AND something else terrible could happen. And hearing that in the moment is hurtful because you're essentially being told, "You shouldn't feel the way you feel right now."

However, what's tricky here is that putting things into perspective should and does work as an emotion hack. This strategy involves reframing situations to include the broader context. This could include reframing negative comments from a supervisor by remembering that it's just one piece of feedback and that other evaluations have been positive. Or, when you're slowed down at a fast-food outlet, remembering that this is a small annoyance in the grand scheme of things.

We have lots of evidence that learning to consider the broader context is an effective way to manage your feelings. In fact, this is one of the regulation strategies measured by the Cognitive Emotion Regulation Questionnaire (CERQ) I discussed in Hack 27, and it's found to be negatively correlated with depression, anxiety and stress. The more people endorsed thoughts such as "This could have been much worse" or "There

---

[14]   Variations of this insensitivity include, "It's only a [game, job, test]," "At least you have [a job, your health, a home]," "It's not a big deal," and "You should be grateful."

are worse things in life," the less depressed, anxious and stressed they got.[15]

Don't Deny Your Feelings

There are a few things that will make embracing putting things into perspective easier and more productive. First, much like positive reappraisal (Hack 27), you want to come to this conclusion on your own instead of having someone tell you. It simply does not feel good to have a person communicate essentially, "Your problems are not that significant" at a time when you really need their support. Second, you likely need a little bit of time to emote before trying to make this shift. Trying to abruptly shift to the broader context too soon after the trigger might be another way of denying your feelings instead of embracing them.

Finally, whether you're encouraging yourself or other people, you want to make sure you don't express this idea in a toxic way. Common refrains such as, "It could be worse" or "It's not a big deal" or "It's only a game" end up hurting more than they help. Although slight variations of these thoughts might work better. Try shifting to something like, "This feels really difficult right now, but in the long run it probably won't feel as bad," or perhaps, "I know you worked really hard on this, but one [game, poor performance, etc.] doesn't define you."

How to Put Things into Perspective

This emotion hack can be really valuable if done well. Here are a few strategies to try to embrace it in the moment.

[15]   Interestingly, putting something into perspective doesn't seem to decrease anger in the same way, probably because anger is so often about justice and fairness. Basically, if you are angry about being treated unfairly, telling yourself that other people have been treated even more unfairly doesn't necessarily make it feel better.

- **Ask yourself if this will matter in the long term:** When faced with a stressful or frustrating situation, pause and question whether this issue will still feel important a year from now. A simple mental shift like this can help reduce emotional intensity and prevent overreacting to relatively minor setbacks.

- **Adopt a third-person perspective:** Try to look at the situation from the perspective of a friend and even consider how you might advise a friend dealing with it. A reframe like this can create some much-needed distance from your immediate emotions and encourage a different way of thinking.

- **Take a moment to zoom out:** When emotions are running high, try to visualize your current situation as a small piece of your overall life story. Recognizing the bigger picture can help shift focus away from immediate frustration and toward long-term growth.

- **Embrace gratitude intentionally:** Try to make actively recognizing the good things in your life, even in difficult moments, a habit. Too often we try to force gratitude on ourselves as a way of suppressing negative feelings. Instead, acknowledge both the real struggles and the real positives in your life.

These four strategies can go a long way toward helping you put things into perspective in a way that is healthy rather than toxic.

Hack 30: Refocus on the Positive

The Uncomfortable Water-Sprayer-Thingy

So far, I've discussed four different positive[16] ways to reframe negative experiences in the moment: refocus on planning (Hack 20), embrace positive reappraisal (Hack 27), use acceptance appropriately (Hack 28) and put things into perspective (Hack 29). I'm adding one more to this list, refocus on the positive, which is when you intentionally think about pleasant or joyful experiences instead of the negative thing that's happened. You shift your focus away from the upsetting trigger and toward thinking about more positive experiences.

I was at the dentist last week and for some reason the high-pitched sound of the water-sprayer-thingy[17] was really getting to me. I've never liked that sound, but it's never affected me like this before. It was becoming really uncomfortable, especially as it got closer to my ears. So, I did what I could to focus on more pleasant thoughts (e.g., a recent vacation) to take me away from the present moment.

I wrote about a similar concept earlier with Hack 6, Embrace Healthy Distraction. Refocusing on the positive is a little different. With distraction, you're *doing* something different so as not to focus on the upsetting stimulus (e.g., going for a walk, losing yourself in work). Distraction is mostly an external strategy where you essentially keep yourself busy. With positive refocus, we have an internal cognitive strategy where you turn your thoughts to more positive but unrelated ones. You shift your thoughts, not your actions.

---

[16]   I describe them as positive only because the research shows that they are typically associated with better psychological outcomes (e.g., lower stress, less anxiety). It's undeniable that they could have negative consequences if used too regularly or in the wrong circumstances. As always, context matters.

[17]   I'm pretty sure that's what it's called. No need to fact-check this.

For example, you may have had a stressful conversation with a loved one that ends with you feeling angry and sad. You play the conversation over and over in your head (i.e., ruminating) in a way that isn't healthy for you. So, you intentionally shift your thoughts away from that conversation toward something more positive. You start thinking about an upcoming vacation or a joyful memory to take yourself away from the emotional conversation.

Refocusing on the positive is measured in the Cognitive Emotion Regulation Questionnaire (CERQ). Eric Dahlen and I found in our research that, as with similar hacks I have shared (see below for a reminder), this thought type decreases sadness, anxiety, anger and stress. Essentially, refocusing on the positive serves as a buffer against emotional distress.

Summary of the Five Positive Thought Types

To help distinguish between the different positive thought types I have shared, here's a quick breakdown of all five.

- **Refocus on planning (Hack 20):** A problem-solving approach where you think about the steps needed to handle or resolve the situation.
- **Embrace positive reappraisal (Hack 27):** A meaning-making approach where you assign a more positive value to the event in terms of personal growth or learning.
- **Use acceptance appropriately (Hack 28):** An approach rooted in realism where you acknowledge and resign yourself to the fact that the event has happened and can't be changed.
- **Put things into perspective (Hack 29):** A severity-reducing approach where you downplay the seriousness of the event by reminding yourself of worse things that have happened.

- **Refocus on the positive (Hack 30):** An attention-shifting approach where you think about more joyful or pleasant things instead of the negative event.

Each of these hacks can serve a valuable purpose when it comes to learning to feel healthier emotions in a particular moment. At the same time, each one could be overused, so learning to identify the appropriate context and usage is a critical aspect of managing your emotions.

Healthy Positivity

While refocusing on the positive can be a really valuable approach to emotion management, overuse can be damaging. Here are some strategies to use this hack while avoiding potential toxicity.

- **Have some go-to positives:** Try building a mental library of happy memories or comforting images, almost like a playlist that you can quickly switch on when emotions run high. The more familiar and vivid these positive thoughts are, the easier it will be to shift your focus when you need a break.
- **Be intentional about how long:** Positive refocusing is most helpful when it's used as a temporary strategy and not as an attempt to escape upsetting situations or feelings permanently. Give yourself a set amount of time to step away mentally, then decide when and how to return to the issue.
- **Pair it with other strategies:** Positive refocusing works best when combined with other tools, such as deep breathing, journaling or problem solving. It can regulate your emotions in the moment, making it easier to take action or re-evaluate the situation later.
- **Practice under low stress:** Try using this positive refocusing technique in response to mild stressors first, so

it becomes second nature when bigger or more negative emotions come up for you. Like any skill, it gets stronger the more you practice it and it's best to do that when the stakes are low.

- **Avoid toxic positivity:** Don't try to force yourself to feel good or pretend things are fine when they're not. Positive refocusing is about giving yourself a break, not denying the reality or importance of your feelings.

This last tip is particularly important. You should think of your emotions as signals that provide you with information about your circumstances or values. Thus, ignoring them or entirely shifting away from them is fundamentally unhealthy. The goal here shouldn't be to suppress feelings but to manage them in a way that serves your ability to listen to them.

Hack 31: Don't Make It About You

Taking Things Personally

A friend of mine recently posted a photo on Instagram. It was a picture of her at work, showing off a project she'd been involved in that was near completion. She was really excited about it, but a day later she came to me and said that her boss hadn't "liked" it, and she felt that must be intentional. She said, "I think she must be disappointed in it. Or maybe she thinks I shouldn't have told anyone about it yet." But then a day later, her boss both liked it and commented, "Proud of you!"

So, for two days my friend obsessed about whether her boss was upset or disappointed with her, only to find out that she hadn't even seen the post yet. My friend was making it all about her when it absolutely wasn't about her. We have a name for this and it's "personalization", which is where we interpret events and behaviors as being specifically directed at us without any real evidence to support that claim. We take things personally, assuming people's actions are motivated by some sort of dislike of or hostility toward us.

You might see this play out in situations at work (e.g., a colleague didn't respond to your email quickly enough, so you decide they are trying to make you look bad) or in social situations (e.g., you find out two friends went to lunch without you and you assume they must have deliberately decided to exclude you). It certainly happens in romantic relationships, especially early on. Your partner doesn't get back to you right away and you assume they are mad at you. They seem quiet one night and you are sure they're losing interest.

All these behaviors have alternative explanations, though. Your colleague might be swamped at work and slow to get through their emails. Your friends may have made those plans last minute and didn't include you for practical reasons. Your partner may have been preoccupied with some unrelated problem that they didn't want to trouble you with. In each case, you're making something personal that may have had very little, if anything, to do with you.

Internalizing Responsibility

Personalization is a natural and even healthy thing to do in early development. In childhood, it's called "egocentric thinking" and it's an expected part of cognitive and emotional development. As kids develop their sense of themselves (i.e., as they figure out how the world works and what role they play in it), they often assume their actions are responsible for the things that happen around them. When Mom or Dad gets angry, they wonder what they did to cause it. It's developmentally normal at this stage because they simply don't have the cognitive capacity to see things from another person's perspective.

Over time, most kids start to realize what they are, and are not, responsible for. But some children continue to internalize that responsibility and it becomes a cognitive habit that is unintentionally reinforced by ambiguous emotional situations. For example, when Mom is emotional, the child thinks, "Mom is mad, so I must have done something wrong. I'll be extra-good to make up for it." Mom naturally appreciates the good behavior and she shows it through positive emotions, reinforcing the child's perspective that it was their behavior that caused the emotions in the first place.

When this type of thinking becomes a habit – when people exhibit a pattern of personalization – it can lead to unnecessary sadness, anxiety and anger. For example, in 2017, researchers explored this issue by evaluating patients with social anxiety disorder as compared to a control group of participants who did not have the disorder.[xxx]

They found that the tendency to personalize was 50 per cent higher in the group with social anxiety disorder. As part of the study, the researchers looked at those socially anxious patients who had symptoms of depression too, and found that they also were much more likely to exhibit personalizing thought patterns.

Minimizing Personalization

As we know personalization is a relatively negative and unhealthy thought habit associated with a host of negative-feeling emotions, it's important to identify ways to minimize it. Here are some strategies.

- **Name it when you recognize it:** When you catch yourself personalizing something, label it for yourself as personalization. Naming the pattern as it's happening is a good first step toward shifting your thinking.
- **Pause and consider other explanations:** Before reacting, take a moment to think why else this might be happening. Intentionally considering other explanations helps to take the focus off yourself.
- **Reality-test with a person you trust:** Share your interpretation with someone who might be able to help you see the situation accurately. An outside perspective can provide additional context that will be helpful to you emotionally.
- **Ask questions:** Instead of assuming intentions, seek clarification when you can. Asking honest questions, especially in a non-defensive way, can help you avoid any misinterpretations.
- **Focus on self-worth:** The better your self-esteem, the less likely you are to assume that others' actions are about you. Building up your self-worth can provide a buffer against this sort of internalizing.

It's worth noting, once again, that the goal isn't to minimize those things that really are personal. While it's unhealthy to assume things are about you when they aren't, it's also a problem to assume that things *aren't* about you when they are. You want your thoughts to match the reality of a situation as closely as possible.

Hack 32: Don't Expect Changed Behavior

We Are All Complicated, Autonomous Beings

Often working in tandem with a tendency to personalize (*see* Hack 31) is a tendency to expect others to change their ways for us. Another potentially problematic thought type, this pattern emerges when we believe that other people (e.g., friends, family, co-workers, romantic partners) should or will change to meet our expectations. For example, imagine you have a friend who tends to give you a lot of advice. You go to this friend to vent sometimes and instead of listening and empathizing, she quickly gravitates toward telling you what you should do. You've told her that this bothers you, but she continues to do it.

On the one hand, it seems totally fair for you to want your friend to adjust how she handles these situations. You've shared with her that it bothers you, so why won't she change? On the other hand, your friend is an autonomous human being with similarly complicated feelings and thoughts, rooted in her own developmental history, who can't necessarily just shift how she behaves because you want her to. She may not have the skill to change, she may not realize how important it is to you, you may not have given the feedback clearly enough or she may not have the self-awareness to realize when it's happening.

"She obviously doesn't value our friendship"

What makes this even more emotionally challenging is that these expectations so often accompany personalization. When your friend doesn't change her behavior, it's easy to think, "She doesn't value this friendship" or "She doesn't respect me." These thoughts seem totally reasonable to you because you're approaching the situation purely from the perspective of, "I asked her to change. This is important to me, and I told her so, so she should change."

In some ways, this connects to Hack 24, Check the Entitlement. Demandingness and entitlement are when you place your own needs and preferences above the needs and preferences of other people. It's when you elevate your desires into these dictatorial demands. These expectations of change could be considered a type of entitlement. Although, it's a little more personal as it often occurs within the context of a close relationship – it would be particularly odd to expect strangers to change for us.

It's the personal nature of these feelings that exacerbates some of the negative emotions that result from them. If your interpretation is, "She won't change because she doesn't respect me," you are no longer just responding to the lack of desired change; you're responding to the more painful feeling that your friend doesn't respect you. If you don't take time to consider the broader circumstances from your friend's perspective – if you personalize the lack of effort – you're likely to feel even more emotional discomfort.

Check Your Expectations

Making some intentional shifts in thinking can help you break out of this pattern of expectation, disappointment and negative emotion. Here are some tips for restructuring some of those unhelpful thoughts.

- **Name and assess the expectation:** Start by clearly identifying for yourself what you're expecting from the other person and do your best to be specific. Part of that includes asking yourself whether that expectation is realistic and fair of you to want from another person.

- **Communicate clearly:** Avoid relying on hints and indicate what you want clearly and concisely. Clear, calm and direct communication allows the other person to consider the request and respond to it. They get the chance to think through what you're asking of them, clarify things they might be confused about and explain what they're thinking about it.
- **Evaluate from their perspective and acknowledge their autonomy:** Do what you can to see the situation through the other person's eyes to better understand what's motivating their behavior and the challenges they might be facing. Even if you can't fully understand it from their perspective, recognizing their autonomy will give you a better grasp of what they can and can't change.
- **Concede that you can't always expect change:** It's important to realize that other people simply may be unwilling or unable to embrace the change you want. Accepting that as reality is a critical step to better managing your feelings here.
- **Be honest about what you're willing to accept:** Knowing your own limits will allow you to make decisions about how to move forward. While you may not be able to expect another person to change, you can consider what your relationship with that person should be, including whether you want to have a relationship with them at all.

Managing the expectation that others will change for you is about shifting the way you think. When you name expectations, communicate directly, respect the autonomy of others and stay honest about your own limits, you protect your emotional wellbeing and build healthier relationships.

Hack 33: Avoid Considering Opinions as Fact

When Opinions Feel Like Attacks

When my oldest son was nine years old, we went to the drive-in movie theater to see the new live-action *Aladdin* movie. He loved it.[18] It's not a great movie, but there was a lot of good dancing, singing and some fun effects. For a nine-year-old, it was a really great ride and seeing it outside at the drive-in made for a great memory. However, on the drive home, we decided to listen to a podcast about the movie and the hosts of that particular show ... did not love *Aladdin*. They were pretty critical of a lot of the things in the movie that my son had loved and he got more and more agitated as he listened to them. Understandably, he didn't like that people were criticizing something he'd enjoyed so much.

This is an example of considering your opinions as facts. It's when you treat your personal beliefs, interpretations or assumptions as if they are objective truths. Instead of recognizing that your thoughts reflect a subjective perspective, you assume that what you think or feel must be true. In this case, "I enjoyed this movie" became "This movie is definitively good," so when other people said, "I did not enjoy this movie," it felt like an attack. You might expect this of a nine-year-old. They're still learning to understand that different people see different things in art or have individual needs and wants that inform their own perspectives. The ability to recognize that your opinion isn't fact is developed through these moments when you hear other people's perspectives.

---

[18]   I suspect he would deny this now, by the way. So if you're reading this, Rhys, trust me. You loved it.

Two Ways We Consider Opinions as Facts

Considering your opinion as fact is associated with two thought subtypes: (1) *mindreading as fact* and (2) *preference as universal truth*. When we mindread as fact, we assume we understand what other people are thinking and then we treat that assumption as though it's a truth. When someone doesn't text us back right away, we might assume they're mad at us. Instead of considering alternatives (e.g., they're busy), we treat that assumption as if it's definitely accurate. Emotionally, this leads to feelings of anxiety and insecurity based on what might be an inaccurate understanding of the situation. You feel sad or hurt because your friend is mad at you even though they might not actually be mad at you.

The second thought subtype, preference as universal truth, is when we assume that something we appreciate (e.g., a favorite show, restaurant, movie) is appreciated by everyone. "I loved this book" becomes "Everyone should love this book," and you feel frustrated, judged or even invalidated when other people don't agree. This second type plays out regularly in politics where an appreciation for a particular candidate or even a particular policy is thought to be the universally correct decision. "I'm going to vote for ... " becomes "How could anyone not vote for ... " and you feel hurt and invalidated when people don't agree with you.

What's the Evidence?

There are some strategies you can embrace to catch yourself in the act of considering your opinions as facts. Here are some ways to shift your thoughts that can lead to less hurt, insecurity and anger.

- **Look for evidence:** Before you accept an opinion as fact, ask yourself what concrete evidence supports it. This is helpful, especially, when you might be mindreading as fact. If your only proof that someone is mad at you is how you're feeling or the assumptions you're making, you're probably considering an opinion as fact.
- **Label the thought:** Take a moment to identify your thought as a judgment, a worry, an assumption, a prediction, etc. By labeling it, you can better recognize when you are treating an opinion as a fact.
- **Use "I think" statements:** If you replace your absolutist language with an "I think" statement, you're reminding yourself that it's an opinion. So instead of saying, "*Aladdin* is great," you say, "I think *Aladdin* is great," and it's clearer to you that the statement isn't fact, but opinion.
- **Imagine explaining the situation to a neutral party:** If you were to describe this situation to a person with no attachment or connection to it, how would you frame it? This is useful if you're dealing with mindreading because it helps strip away some of the emotional bias you might be feeling.

When you don't check a tendency to consider opinions as fact, you get locked into a way of thinking in which your emotions are based on incomplete or incorrect information. These four strategies can help you recognize what you're doing and shift your thinking away from conjecture to reality.

Hack 34: Don't Dismiss Positives

Reinforcing Negative Views

In 2009, researchers designed a series of studies to explore the impact of positive self-statements on mood.[xxxi] In one of the studies, the researchers split the participants into two groups based on low and high self-esteem. They then randomly assigned participants to do one of the following: either (1) repeat positive self-statements (e.g., "I am a lovable person") to themselves every 15 seconds for 4 minutes, or (2) write about their thoughts and feelings during that time instead, without making the self-statements.

Participants were later assessed on their mood and self-esteem, with researchers likely hoping that repeating these sorts of positive affirmations would increase self-esteem. What they found, though, was more complicated. The participants with low self-esteem actually felt worse after four minutes of making positive self-statements. They were in a worse mood emotionally and their self-esteem decreased. This didn't happen with the high self-esteem group; they felt better. What seems to have happened is that the low self-esteem group pushed back on those positive self-statements in a way that made them feel worse. When they told themselves, "I am a lovable person," another voice in their head responded with, "No, I'm not," and ended up reinforcing their negative views.

Ultimately, this study speaks to a thought type known as "dismissing positives", whereby people reject or minimize positive experiences, accomplishments and achievements in favor of a more negative outlook. When they accomplish something, they say, "Well that doesn't count" or "That was just luck." It's a thought habit that keeps you stuck with a negative self-image because you dismiss the good things that happen and cling to the bad things.

Minimizing Accomplishments

Dismissing positives might show up at work, in school or in your relationships. If you get a good grade on an exam, you are quick to think, "I bet everyone did well" or "This professor must be an easy grader." If your boss gives you positive feedback, you might think, "They're just being nice to get me to take on more work." If you meet your health goals by exercising for a month, you might think, "I still have so far to go, this doesn't mean much."

Of course, the emotional toll here is that you don't leave yourself much room for happiness or excitement because you keep minimizing your accomplishments. You end up wallowing in disappointment even when good things happen. Plus, people who dismiss positives rarely dismiss negatives in the same way. When a bad thing happens, they don't say, "Well that was just bad luck" or "That doesn't count." They often embrace negatives as real evidence of who they actually are.

However, something interesting happened in that 2009 study, which was similarly unexpected and speaks to another way of addressing the problem. The researchers split the low self-esteem participants into one of two groups: (1) a positive-focus group where they had to focus only on how the statement "I am a lovable person" was true, and (2) a neutral-focus group where they were allowed to focus on how that statement was true and/or not true. Afterwards, the members of the positive-focus group were found to have a much worse mood and a lower self-esteem than the neutral-focus group. So, being allowed to entertain the possibility that the statement might be either true or false had a more positive impact on the emotions of people with low self-esteem.

It's OK to Have Doubts

If you find yourself dismissing positives this way, you're (a) not alone and (b) not going to find much success in trying to force yourself to believe positive self-statements. If the research has communicated one thing, it's that trying to make people say positives about themselves is unlikely to work. Instead, here are some things you can try.

- **Don't try to force positive beliefs:** If you don't really believe them, your mind will push back even harder. This mental resistance can make you feel worse, not better, especially if the affirmation highlights a gap between where you are and where you want to be. Instead of trying to "overwrite" your feelings, acknowledge them and work with them. Growth starts with honesty, not denial.
- **Listen for "yeah but" thinking:** Pay attention to times when you follow compliments or success with "yeah but ... " That's the type of thinking that typically sets off dismissal of positives, so being able to catch it is a good first step in conquering this negative thought tendency.
- **Accept praise with curiosity:** Instead of attempting to accept all praise, which might be too much at first, try to learn to accept it with curiosity. Start asking yourself, "What if they're right?" You're not forcing yourself to believe the positive thing. You're simply asking yourself to consider the possibility.
- **Keep a proof list:** Some people find it helpful to keep a list of things that contradict their inner critic. It might be praise they've received, things they've done well or their major accomplishments. The key here is to make sure you don't debate the list. You just keep it as a record of things you've done.

Know that it's OK to have doubts about yourself or your abilities. As with the other hacks we've discussed, the goal isn't to delude yourself into believing things that aren't true. What you want is to have accurate thoughts about the situations you're in, the people you engage with and, in this case, your own abilities and accomplishments.

CHAPTER 7
EMOTIONAL FEELING HACKS

Going back to the Why We Feel Model (*see* page 14), the three things we've talked about so far – stimulus, mood at the time and interpretation – all intersect to create the emotional feeling. That emotional feeling includes a host of physiological activations. Your heart rate and breathing increase, your muscles tense up and you start to sweat. This is your body's way of preparing you for some sort of activity (e.g., to fight if you're angry or to flee if you're scared).

Despite their roots in our evolutionary history, these emotional experiences can often feel overwhelming. The release of adrenaline that often accompanies the emotion leaves you with a pounding heart, shaky hands and racing thoughts. That rush can be so intense that it drowns out your ability to think clearly or respond calmly.

Psychologists have identified a variety of strategies to help people learn to calm themselves in those moments. But calming down isn't the only way to handle yourself when highly emotional. Sometimes it's less about calming down and more about listening to your emotions.

In this chapter, I'll talk through a variety of approaches you can try in those emotional moments. They include ways of staying calm, staying focused and remembering what's important to you, as well as a few things you should avoid.

- Hack 35: Be Open to Learning About the Situation
- Hack 36: Be Open to Learning About Yourself
- Hack 37: Ground Yourself
- Hack 38: Have a Mantra
- Hack 39: Ask Yourself if the Feeling Is Valid
- Hack 40: Breathe Deeply
- Hack 41: Embrace Emotional Discomfort
- Hack 42: Practice Mindfulness
- Hack 43: Take a Broader View
- Hack 44: Avoid Exercise and Catharsis

The goal isn't to eliminate emotion but to learn how to stay grounded, present and intentional – even when your body is screaming at you to react.

Hack 35: Be Open to Learning About the Situation

It's OK to Feel Overwhelmed

I have a friend, Jordan,[1] who told me a story about when she moved to Chicago for her new job and found herself feeling really down. There was some homesickness, she said, but it felt like more than that. She wasn't sleeping well and she wasn't enjoying her job. Ultimately, she felt lonely and sad most of the time. She started to unpack that emotion and realized a few things.

Jordan had made this big life change, moving to Chicago and taking a new job far away from her family and friends. The change itself had been exhausting and overwhelming with all the packing, finding a place to live and saying goodbye to her friends. Jordan thought once it all settled, she would be happy and excited, but she wasn't. She was still down. She realized she wasn't just missing people, she was starting to see her sadness as some sort of personal failure. Everyone had told her that moving and taking this job would be great, so the fact that she was struggling made her feel like a disappointment.

So, Jordan made a shift in both her thinking and her behavior. First, she told herself that it was OK to feel overwhelmed and disappointed. That was normal and it was probably unrealistic for her to have expected otherwise. She also decided she needed to be more intentional about connecting with people. She joined a book club through her local library, started volunteering every other week and made a point of calling old friends regularly so she could stay connected. Over time, Jordan started to feel a little more like her old self and started to get excited about her time in Chicago.

---

[1]   Not her real name. But she gave me permission to use this story and I asked her to pick a name. She chose this one because she "had just read a book set in Jordan".

A Source of Useful Information

One of the most powerful things your emotions can do for you is offer insight into your situation. That might sound obvious, but it's easy to overlook, especially when we're overwhelmed, confused or reactive. Emotions often feel like something happening to us. But when we pause and examine them, we recognize that they're important datapoints. They are clues we can use to understand what's going on in our lives, what we value and what we need.

Remember, your emotions emerge from three primary elements: the stimulus, your mood at the time, and your interpretation of what's happening. When we face a situation like the one Jordan faced, we can use that same model to understand more about what's going on. For example, let's say you feel sad after scrolling through social media. As you unpack that situation, you might realize you're thinking, "Everyone else is doing great, and I'm falling behind." Your sadness, then, is partially about what others are doing and partially about how you're interpreting your own situation in comparison. That's useful information. It doesn't mean the sadness is wrong or unimportant, but it does mean there's a path to explore. What might you need to change about your life to feel like you're not falling behind?

Questions to Ask Yourself

Using your emotions to better understand what you're feeling and why you're feeling it requires you to dig deep and give honest answers to tough questions. Here are some things you can ask yourself in emotional moments.

- **What exactly am I feeling right now?** This isn't nearly as simple as it sounds. Sometimes we're feeling just one thing and other times we're feeling a lot of things simultaneously. The first step is to go beyond surface-level understandings and really pay attention to the emotion(s) you're feeling. Is it sadness? Or is it a more nuanced feeling such as grief, yearning, guilt, inadequacy, numbness or hopelessness?

- **What story am I telling myself about this situation?** Given that your emotions are so deeply tied to how you interpret events, asking yourself about the meaning you're assigning to what's happened is key to better understanding it.

- **How would I explain this situation to someone else?** If you were to describe the circumstances to a friend (or even a stranger), how would you explain it? Thinking through that explanation can give you some perspective into what you're feeling and why you're feeling it.

- **What might this emotion be urging me to do and will that be helpful?** Emotions push us toward action. They motivate us to act in a particular way. Part of what we need to do, though, is figure out if that action is the right thing to do. Will that impulse help or will it make things worse?

The best way to think of emotions is to consider them as sources of information. However, you can't think of that information as infallible or 100 per cent accurate. It has to be evaluated to determine what it's really telling you about the situation you're in.

Hack 36: Be Open to Learning About Yourself

Realizing There's a Pattern

In Hack 35, we talked about how emotions can give you useful insight into how you feel about and interpret a situation. But emotions also do something else – they reveal who you are. They reflect your values, your needs and even your personality traits. They don't just tell you about the situation; they tell you about you.

For example, take Marcus, a high school teacher who often finds himself frustrated with his school's leadership. In meetings, he feels like the conversations are going around in circles and nothing concrete is being decided. It's not just mild irritation either. Marcus gets tense, short with colleagues afterwards and is often distracted for the rest of the day. It might seem like simple impatience to a lot of people, but when he takes time to reflect, Marcus sees there's a pattern there. He realizes he feels most frustrated when he believes his time is being wasted or when leadership avoids accountability.

Thinking through this, Marcus can realize that he values clarity, structure and follow-through. He wants to do good work and he wants to be part of a system that functions well. His emotional reactions are signaling that the things he wants – based on those values – aren't being provided. There's also a personality component here. Marcus is a conscientious person and he prefers working where expectations are clear. From this perspective, his frustration isn't random. It's aligned with the kind of person he is. Marcus is someone who takes pride in efficiency and purpose and these values are revealed through his feelings.

What We Care About

In Hack 23, Identify Your Core Beliefs, we discussed the need to know what your deeply held convictions are because they influence your emotions. My argument there was that by identifying and even modifying your core beliefs, you can better manage your emotions. Though the other side of that is that your emotions can help you identify the things that matter to you most. In simple terms, the things we emote about reflect the things we care about, sometimes on a deeply personal level. By paying attention to our emotions, especially to what they tell us about ourselves, we don't just learn to cope a little better, we learn more about what's important to us and what we care about most. That insight can guide us in managing our frustrations and also in better fitting into and navigating the world around us. Someone like Marcus can decide, now that he better understands his own needs and wants, what sort of work environment he needs in order to really thrive.

This notion that your emotions are not random reactions but are actually adaptive and useful is rooted in a functionalist theory of emotions.[xxxii] Your emotions exist because they solve specific problems, either physical or social challenges. They help coordinate your physiological response, your thoughts and your behaviors in solving each problem. So, from that perspective, your feelings show that something meaningful to you is at stake (e.g., a goal, a need, a relationship or a deep personal value).

- **Anger** arises when we perceive that something we value (e.g., fairness, respect, autonomy) is being violated. It signals that a boundary may have been crossed.
- **Awe** is triggered by beauty or significance that challenges our normal ways of understanding. It reveals that we have a deep appreciation of something.

- **Curiosity** signals a gap in our knowledge that we might find valuable, surprising or useful. It drives us to learn or explore.
- **Disgust** exists to protect us from contamination, not just physical but also moral or social. It signals that something violates our sense of purity or integrity.
- **Fear** emerges when we perceive a threat, often physical, but can include more existential threats and can help us understand what things really matter most to us (e.g., safety, reputation).
- **Guilt** signals that we've done something that conflicts with our values, so highlights the values we hold most dear.
- **Joy** happens when something in our wants and needs is met, so feeling joy reinforces what we want most in the world.
- **Sadness** is triggered by loss – a person, an object or even an opportunity. It reveals what was most meaningful to us.

Six Questions to Ask Yourself

Of course, the fact that your emotions might mean something about your values and identity is only useful to you if you are skilled at identifying those core convictions. Here are six questions you can ask yourself to get to the bottom of your core convictions.

1. **What does this emotion seem to be protecting?** Our feelings often show up when something important feels threatened. This reaction might be defending your self-worth, your boundaries, a relationship or a belief you hold dear.
2. **What am I afraid I might lose?** Fear, sadness or even anger can point to a deeper anxiety about losing something that matters (e.g., respect, control, connection, opportunity). Identifying that potential loss can help clarify what you value most in the moment.

3. **What expectations or desires do I have that aren't being met?** So often, our emotional responses are fueled by unmet hopes or unspoken expectations. Asking this question helps you recognize the gap between what you wanted and what actually happened.

4. **If someone else were feeling this way, what might I assume they care about?** Taking a step back and imagining someone else in your shoes can give you some perspective. It might reveal the underlying value or need (e.g., fairness, loyalty, validation) that's driving your emotional response.

5. **Is this emotion telling me something about the kind of person I want to be?** This is a biggie. Emotions can reflect your internal standards. For example, guilt might mean you want to be more honest, or pride might reinforce a desire to be dependable. Your feelings are often about how your values shape your identity.

6. **What would need to change in this situation for me to feel better?** This question can help shift your focus from the emotion to the value behind it. The change you imagine (e.g., more respect, more clarity, more connection) often reveals the unmet need or principle at the heart of your response.

Taken together, our emotions aren't just a feeling state we need to deal with or get over. When we listen closely to them – not only for what they say about the situation but for what they reveal about our values, needs and identity – we can learn to better understand ourselves.

Hack 37: Ground Yourself

A Hard Time Thinking Straight

I once spoke to a woman named Chris about some pretty intense anger outbursts she was having, often in response to arguments she had with her husband.[2] She told me she once got so angry with him that she threw the lid from a large plastic bin across the room, and that it hit the wall and shattered into hundreds of pieces. As we talked about it, Chris explained that her anger actually stemmed from her anxiety.[3] She said she would get anxious and have a hard time thinking straight or accomplishing anything or even feeling at ease. All that discomfort would lead to frustration and anger. Chris would yell, throw things and regularly snap at people – usually her husband.

Through therapy, Chris was diagnosed with generalized anxiety disorder and she started to better understand a lot of her anxiety triggers (e.g., getting in trouble at work, disputes at home,[4] possible car accidents). She also learned a whole bunch of strategies for managing both the anxiety and the anger. One that Chris found particularly helpful was

[2]   I interviewed Chris for my first book, *Why We Get Mad* (2021), and her story has stuck with me.

[3]   Much to my frustration, people often describe anger as a "secondary emotion," arguing that it always stems from some other feeling such as fear or sadness. It can be secondary, like with Chris, but it isn't always secondary. Frankly, the argument that anger is inherently a secondary emotion is really minimizing to people who have very real things to be angry about.

[4]   One of the most interesting things about Chris's story was how her husband inadvertently made her feel so much worse. In his rush to help her, he would say things like, "Everything's fine," which ended up feeling minimizing to her. It was the emotional equivalent of telling her to relax, which made it feel like he didn't take her concerns seriously and led to anger and conflict.

grounding, which is an emotion-management strategy that helps people anchor themselves in the present moment. It's especially useful for people like Chris who are often overwhelmed by intense emotions.

The Five Senses Approach

Grounding can look a lot of ways, but what Chris found most helpful was what she called the five senses approach, where she would think of:

- five things she could see
- four things she could feel
- three things she could hear
- two things she could smell
- one thing she could taste.

Chris said, "By the time you get down to that one thing, you've kind of distracted your mind from the anxiety and you're focused on things that are tangible."

This is but one of quite a few grounding techniques people use to interrupt an emotional cycle before it escalates. Given that the goal of these techniques is to connect with the present moment, most of them are sensing techniques such as the one above. Sometimes people will hold on to something textured such as a rock or a piece of fabric. Or maybe they'll intentionally smell a strong scent such as oil or coffee grounds. They might walk barefoot through the grass or just plant their feet firmly on the ground. Even splashing water on your face could be considered a grounding technique. The core idea of all of these is to shift your attention away from distressing internal experiences (e.g., racing thoughts, traumatic memories, overwhelming emotions) and toward the external, physical world.

Learning to Ground Yourself

Grounding can be an effective approach for minimizing unwanted emotions in the moment. It works best, though, when it's a habit. To that end, here are four steps you can take to add this practice to your life.

1. **Identify a grounding approach that works for you.** As there are a few different grounding techniques, it makes sense to experiment with approaches until you find something that works for you. I like the five senses technique because it can be done anywhere and without needing any objects, but you should use the one that works best for you.
2. **Use your chosen approach regularly, especially before stressful moments.** Try to make grounding part of a routine so it becomes second nature. One goal should be to use it proactively instead of purely reactively. Try to ground yourself before events or activities you anticipate being emotional (e.g., before a difficult conversation, an important meeting at work, an exam).
3. **Learn to stop yourself in the moment.** When your emotions are escalating, work on catching yourself. Even a few seconds of pause and grounding can interrupt a spiral, helping you respond with intention instead of reacting from feeling overwhelmed.
4. **Reflect and adjust.** Take time to reflect on whether your grounding technique is working the way you want it to and adjust as necessary. Asking yourself if it worked, what helped and what didn't help can refine this important skill.

Grounding can be an important emotion-management technique, but it will work best if you think of it as a skill that you practice regularly. By working on it, especially in calm moments, you'll be better equipped to stay steady when life gets intense.

Hack 38: Have a Mantra

"Prolonged repetitive verbal utterances"

In 2015, five researchers from the Department of Neurobiology at the Weizmann Institute of Science in Israel[xxxiii] set out to better understand the neurological impact of "prolonged repetitive verbal utterances."[5] They did this by having 23 participants silently repeat the word "one" for several minutes while having an fMRI (functional magnetic resonance imaging) brain scan. They selected the word "one" specifically because they wanted a word that had no spiritual or meditative connotations, in order to isolate the effects of repetitive speech alone rather than involving the meaning of the word itself. Therefore, the researchers selected a neutral word without any associated symbolism or emotions, and then made comparisons to participants who were just resting or generating words on their own.

You may remember from Hack 25, where we discussed rumination, that the default mode network (DMN) is a set of brain structures associated with daydreaming and mind wandering. This is the network you want to disrupt or deactivate to decrease the experience of unwanted emotions. What these researchers found was that repeating the word "one" over and over led to a significant reduction of brain activity in the DMN.

This is in contrast to what happened to the other participants. When they were resting, their DMN was active, which makes sense because that's when mind wandering and daydreaming would normally happen. When participants were generating their own set of words, there was some decreased

---

5   There's almost nothing I find funnier than academic jargon. Somehow, people decided the phrase "prolonged repetitive verbal utterances" was a better choice of words than "saying something over and over."

activation in the DMN, but there was activity in the particular areas associated with language (again, as you would expect given the task). Taken together, this study suggests that word repetition is a really effective way to quiet your mind.

Mantras – Another Form of Grounding

Part of what's interesting about the 2015 study is that the researchers specifically selected a word that has little emotive or symbolic meaning, so it is the activity of repeating something to yourself that is itself valuable. Now add to that the potential benefits of selecting a phrase that has some additional meaning, either because it's inspiring or spiritual or serves as a reminder of some core value. When you use a mantra – a short, repeatable phrase that's designed to help you regulate your emotions – you may give the act of repetition additional power.

In some ways, your mantra can serve as another tool that grounds you, redirects your focus and reminds you of your values or goals when your emotions start to feel overwhelming. It's different from an affirmation, which might be about self-worth or positivity (e.g., "I am enough," "I deserve good things.") A good mantra is typically functional. It serves to disrupt unhelpful emotional reactions and cue a healthier emotional response. For example:

- "Just breathe."
- "Be present."
- "Let go."
- "I don't need to win this."
- "I don't need to carry this."
- "Pause. Breathe. Choose."
- "Protect my peace."

A good mantra can do a few different things to help manage

emotions. It can serve to regulate your physiology (as the study above showed). It can prompt particular behaviors or ways of thinking by reminding you what you want to do in these moments or by replacing unhealthy thoughts with more adaptive ones. It can also remind you what kind of person you want to be, by encouraging you to reconnect with your identity.

Selecting a Mantra

As I was writing this, I asked people on social media if they had a mantra, and if so, what was it. I received a lot of really interesting answers, ranging from common phrases such as "This too shall pass" to people quoting scripture. Though what is fascinating is how often people select a wording that is about accepting situations (e.g., "What is meant for me will come to me") rather than a cue or command to take you in a new direction (e.g., "Walk it off").

To create a good mantra, ask yourself a few things.

1. **What situations/emotions do you most need this for?** The mantra you use to deal regularly with fear or anxiety might be different from the words you use to deal regularly with anger or sadness.
2. **What will I remember in the moment?** A mantra is only going to be successful if it comes naturally to you and you are able to remember it when you need it. You should pick something short, focused and personal.
3. **What tone are you looking for?** Any self-statement should match the tone you're trying to achieve in that moment (e.g., calming, empowering, humorous), so select something that's consistent with what you're trying to achieve.

A mantra isn't going to be a panacea, but it might be just the thing you need in an emotional moment to help you refocus and regulate.

Hack 39: Ask Yourself if the Feeling Is Valid

A Not at All Bold but Still Controversial Claim

I'm going to start this hack with a claim that I think is really obvious but still seems to be controversial ... at least on social media. That claim is that our emotions are not necessarily valid.

To be clear, our emotions are *real*. They *exist*. They're *important* and we should pay attention to them. But none of those things make them *valid*.

Of course, some of this is rooted in how we're defining validity, so let me break this down for you. Emotional validity is the extent to which an emotional response is reasonable, justifiable and proportionate to the situation that triggered it. For an emotion to be valid, it needs to make some sense given the context and it needs to align with the reality of the situation. It shouldn't be rooted in distorted or inaccurate thinking, unresolved personal issues or unreasonable fears. This is important because while your feelings in a given situation might be real and important and meaningful to you, they aren't necessarily grounded in an accurate interpretation of events, or fair to the others in the situation.

It's not hard to find examples of emotions that are rooted in distorted or inaccurate thinking. For example, specific phobias are defined in the *Diagnostic and Statistical Manual of Mental Disorders*[xxxiv] as fears that are "out of proportion to the actual danger", so they are by definition excessive. Likewise, people often report excessive and even problematic jealousy when their partners have friends they deem too close. Meanwhile, a common thread on mental health social media is people feel excessive guilt for setting personal boundaries. All these feelings are real and relatively common but not necessarily rooted in healthy, accurate thinking.

This has proved to be a hard thing to get people to consider over the last few years. There's been so much focus in popular psychology on the importance of validating our feelings that a lot of people have become reluctant to admit that some feelings are unreasonable. There are two reasons why this is a problem. First, part of being an emotionally mature person is to do the difficult work of evaluating the validity of your emotions. You need to ask yourself if your feelings are coming from a healthy place. Second, thinking that all emotions are valid can actually be dangerous.

A Control Tactic

To explore this second issue further, "my emotions are valid" can and has been used – intentionally or unintentionally – as an abuse and control tactic. For example, take the romantic partner who says, "It makes me uncomfortable when you [spend so much time with your friends, post pictures of yourself on social media, dress provocatively]." Statements like these are often couched in the idea that their discomfort is valid and therefore the other person needs to stop doing whatever they are doing. Instead, perhaps the uncomfortable person should take a moment to ask themselves:

- Why am I uncomfortable with them spending time with their friends?
- Why do I get uneasy when they post pictures on social media or dress provocatively?
- Is this discomfort coming from a reasonable, healthy place?

Now, the person who voices these concerns probably really is uncomfortable. Those feelings are real and they are worth exploring. But, we have to keep two things in mind here: (1) being real isn't the same as being valid and (2) being invalid doesn't make them unimportant.

Invalid Feelings Still Matter

You can learn a lot about yourself and your situation by exploring your emotions when they come from an unreasonable or unhealthy place. For example, if you get uncomfortable when your partner posts a picture of themselves on social media, that likely means something about how secure you feel in your relationship. If you're feeling a lot of guilt for setting what most would consider appropriate boundaries at work, it might mean something about your sense of responsibility. These are important things to consider and we hold ourselves back by not doing the work of interrogating them.

Think of your emotions as signals – important messages about how you're experiencing the world. But like any signal, they're not always accurate. Sometimes they reflect deep truths about your needs or values. Other times they're shaped by past wounds, cognitive errors or unreasonable expectations. That's why emotional intelligence isn't just about feeling your emotions, it's about investigating them.

When you feel something strongly, don't immediately assume that the emotion is justified, helpful or that others are obligated to respond to it the way you want. Instead, pause and do the reflective work. Ask yourself:

1. **Where is this feeling coming from?** Is it about the current situation or is it being amplified by past experiences, unmet needs or unresolved fears?
2. **Why am I feeling this way?** What specific thoughts, assumptions or interpretations are fueling this emotion? What story am I telling myself right now that's leading to this feeling?
3. **What does this emotion say about me?** Is it pointing to a value I care deeply about? Or does it reveal insecurity, fear or a desire to control?

4. **Is this a problem I need to solve internally or something that needs to change externally?** Do I need to change my perspective or behavior – or is this a sign that someone else's actions are truly crossing a line?

Taking the time to ask these questions doesn't make your feelings any less real – it just helps you figure out whether they're valid, actionable and fair. Anything less is a shortcut that risks you hurting yourself or the people around you.

Hack 40: Breathe Deeply

Emotion Physiology 101

Your brain has an extraordinarily sophisticated way of responding to threats and provocations. When you take in information that you perceive as dangerous, your amygdala (the emotion-processing center of the brain) sends a message to the hypothalamus, which initiates the sympathetic nervous system, otherwise known as the fight-or-flight system.

This is what prepares your body for action by releasing adrenaline, increasing your heart rate, speeding up your breathing, tensing your muscles, dilating your pupils and slowing down your digestion. Essentially, your body is activating for a fight and so does all the things necessary to make you the strongest, while also conserving energy by shutting down the things – such as digestion – that are not necessary in that moment.

This is useful and adaptive when there's actual danger, but modern life doesn't present us with actual danger that often. Instead, we are presented with far less dangerous, but still irritating, provocations such as annoying emails, traffic jams and online political disputes. These things don't require physical action, but we're still responding to them physiologically as if they are a threat from the distant past.

Twenty Minutes to Recover

After the sympathetic nervous system prepares you for action, your parasympathetic nervous system – often called the rest-and-digest system – helps bring you back down to a more balanced state. Here, your heart rate decreases, your digestive system restarts and your muscles relax. It takes approximately 20 minutes to come down from that fight-or-flight state, but there are things you can do to intentionally trigger the parasympathetic nervous system. One of those is deep breathing.

When you're stressed, upset or emotional, your breathing often becomes shallow and rapid, which sends signals to your brain that something is wrong. To counter that, you can take deep, intentional breaths, which will send the opposite message. This signals that you're safe and can calm down. The result is a decrease in heart rate and an overall sense of control over your emotional and physiological state.

For example, there will be times during my day when I realize I'm a little bit frantic internally. My mind will be racing and I'll have a hard time focusing on just one thing.[6][xxxv] When I catch myself in those moments, what works best is to pause and tell myself to focus, and then take a deep, intentional breath. I repeat this as necessary until I'm ready to move on in a more focused way.

Four Ways to Breathe Deeply

Deep breathing is one of the quickest ways to interrupt an unwanted emotional spiral and restore balance. You can use deep breathing in two ways: (1) when emotional and/or (2) regularly throughout your day. In the first approach, when you recognize yourself becoming anxious, angry or otherwise tense, you can take a few moments to engage in deep breathing.

---

[6] My friend Jennie calls this being a "Chaos Muppet," which is a reference to a 2012 article in *Slate* magazine by Dahlia Lithwick. The article argues that every living human can be classified as either a Chaos Muppet or an Order Muppet. I'm clearly an Order Muppet – highly regimented and uncomfortable with surprises. That said, I definitely fall into mental chaos sometimes that likens me far more to the Chaos Muppets (e.g., Ernie, Cookie Monster, Grover). I guess what I'm saying is that I subscribe to a state-trait theory of Muppetry.

Alternatively, you can simply schedule times throughout your day to use deep breathing more as a preventative measure.

Regardless of the approach, there are a few different deep-breathing strategies you can use. Here are four of them. Give each a try and stick with the one that works best for you.

- **Box breathing:** Inhale for a count of 4, hold for a count of 4, exhale for a count of 4 and hold for another count of 4. Then repeat. Those moments of holding your breath are really important because they slow things down for you in a way that allows you to increase your focus.
- **Triangle breathing:** Inhale for a count of 4, hold for a count of 4 and exhale for another count of 4, then repeat without the final hold. This is similar to box breathing, but letting go of that final hold makes it feel a little more natural for some people.
- **4-7-8 breathing:** Inhale for a count of 4, hold for a count of 7 and exhale for a count of 8. The longer exhale here is a valuable approach for triggering the parasympathetic nervous system because it helps to activate the vagus nerve that runs from your brainstem to your abdomen.
- **Diaphragmatic breathing:** Often called "belly breathing," here you want to be intentional about breathing deeply into your abdomen, watching your belly rise and then exhaling slowly. This also helps engage the vagus nerve to stimulate relaxation.

Deep breathing is one of the most valuable hacks in your emotion-management hackpack. It's simple, easy, free, can be done anywhere and its impact on your emotional health can be profound, especially if you practice it regularly.

Hack 41: Embrace Emotional Discomfort

"He's scared of public speaking"

On the first day of the first class I ever taught, I had a student leave about ten minutes into class and never come back. He took the syllabus when I passed it out, read through it, got up, left and dropped the class. I was a graduate student at the time and I told my advisor about it and he said, "I think I know that student," and then asked me their name. I told him and he said, "Yeah, that's who I thought. He's scared of public speaking. He probably saw you had presentations and decided to drop the class. He's done that before."

An important note here is that the presentations I had in that class were as short and simple as they come. It was a five-minute talk with lots of prep and practice time. Plus, it was not a large class so it would have been a small and probably forgiving audience. If ever there was an opportunity to learn to be comfortable with public speaking, it was in this class. He would have been better off sticking with the class and pushing through the discomfort.

Now, I'm certain there's at least someone reading this who is thinking, "But if it was a true phobia, he might just not have been able to do it!" Or maybe someone else is thinking, "But he didn't want to, so why not drop the class in favor of a class where he doesn't have to?" To the first point I would say, I'm sure it was a true phobia but I'm also sure he would have been able to do the presentation if he *needed* to or was given more of an incentive. I'm quite sure if someone said, "Here's $10 million to do a 5-minute talk for 14 people," he would have found a way to push through the emotional discomfort and do the talk. So it wasn't an issue of *can't*, it was an issue of *really didn't want to*. To the second point, I admit this is a value judgment, but being able to speak publicly when you leave college is better than not being able to speak publicly.

The student had held himself back in a significant way by avoiding that particular requirement.

Benefits of Pushing Through

All of this is to say that being able to push through some level of emotional discomfort is a valuable approach to dealing with emotions. Remember back with Hack 4, Select Situations Wisely, when I talked about "thoughtful avoidance." This is why being thoughtful is so important. Always or even often selecting avoidance will lead to further discomfort over time because you never learn to cope with the negative feeling. Avoiding the emotions – whether it's fear, sadness, anger, guilt, etc. – teaches you that the feeling is dangerous or intolerable. You never learn to manage it.

You can liken this to physical exercise where the benefits typically come when you push yourself into some level of discomfort. For example, when you lift weights to the point of fatigue, you create tears in your muscle fibers and your muscles grow stronger as those tears recover. When you engage in intense aerobic exercise, your heart and lungs have to work harder to deliver oxygen, and over time this improves your heart and lung capacity.

When you let yourself feel some anxiety, anger or sadness, you learn that you can cope with it. You develop a certain amount of emotional toughness that allows you to stay calmer under stress. In fact, exposure therapy – where you gradually and repeatedly expose yourself to the thing you're scared of – is a core element of most anxiety disorder treatments. I would argue that it's necessary for the treatment of many fears, especially phobias. As avoidance exacerbates the fear, one of the solutions is to slowly and systematically be exposed to the thing or things you're afraid of.

Being Careful Not to Overdo It

Of course, as with exercise, you can overdo it. You can work out too hard and hurt yourself or just wear yourself down over time by not letting yourself rest. This is true of emotional labor as well and there's two ways this can happen: (1) by carrying too much emotional weight for too long and (2) by exposing yourself to negative emotions that are too intense. The first can lead to emotional exhaustion, which is associated with burnout, depression and anxiety. The second can lead to traumatizing or retraumatizing; for example, if you try to cure your spider phobia by letting spiders crawl all over you, you're probably going to traumatize yourself rather than learn to manage the anxiety.

The goal, then, is to let yourself sit with a small and manageable level of emotional discomfort when you can. Try to avoid distracting yourself completely or avoiding the discomfort altogether, so that you learn to feel that emotion and push through the discomfort. When you feel anxious, remind yourself that the anxiety is normal and even healthy and that you shouldn't let it prevent you from doing the thing you want or need to do.

Hack 42: Practice Mindfulness

A Reciprocal Feedback Loop

In 2017, four researchers set out to explore how different emotion-regulation strategies worked in daily life.[xxxvi] Specifically, they were interested in cognitive reappraisal, suppression and mindfulness. To do this, the researchers had 187 participants complete some baseline surveys on their use of various emotion-regulation approaches and their general mood. For the next 21 days, those participants ended each day with a 5–10-minute survey on their mood and that day's use of those three strategies. What this gave the researchers at the end of those three weeks, then, was an accurate and realistic understanding of how these different emotion-management strategies worked in real life. As this data was relatively in the moment, the researchers were able to assess if mindfulness, for example, impacted daily emotions more or less than suppression or cognitive reappraisal.

The researchers found that mindfulness – paying attention to the present moment in a purposeful and non-judgmental way – was the most consistently beneficial strategy of the three.[7] Cognitive reappraisal, where you intentionally try to change how you think about the situation, worked for most people, but did increase negative emotions for some. Emotional suppression actually had an overall negative impact by increasing negative emotions and decreasing positive emotions. But practicing mindfulness was found to

---

[7] Personally, I find this news devastating. I'm not good at mindfulness. In fact, I'm terrible at it. I want to be good at it. And I've tried to be good at it, but I can't seem to get my brain to focus on the moment. Every time I say this, someone comes along and says something like, "You're thinking about this the wrong way. You need to just be with your thoughts in a non-judgmental way." But that doesn't make any sense to me. You can't tell me to be non-judgmental and tell me I'm doing something wrong in the same breath.

lower negative emotions and increase positive emotions.

The authors were also interested in "spillover effects" – how the use of these strategies impacted participants' feelings the next day. For example, does embracing mindfulness on Tuesday increase positive emotions on Wednesday? Not only that, the researchers wanted to assess directionality to see if how you felt one day impacted what strategies you used the next day. What they found was that mindfulness decreased the likelihood of participants feeling negative emotions the next day. Also, negative emotions meant that people were less likely to use mindfulness the following day, while positive emotions meant that they were more likely to practice it.

All of this means three things.

1. Mindfulness is a valuable emotion-management strategy, decreasing negative emotions and increasing positive ones in the moment.
2. Mindfulness supports longer-lasting emotional wellbeing, predicting emotional wellness even a day after use.
3. Emotional wellness leads to longer-lasting mindfulness, predicting that the strategy will be used the next day.

In other words, not only does mindfulness support emotional wellness, but there's also what we call a "reciprocal feedback loop" whereby mindfulness improves mood and that good mood also supports mindfulness.[8]

Ways to Build Mindfulness into Your Life

You can think about mindfulness in the context of emotion management as (1) planned mindfulness and (2) in-the-moment mindfulness. Both these approaches are valuable emotion hacks.

---

[8]   Fine! I'll try again in a non-judgmental but still sort of judgmental way.

1. **Planned mindfulness:** This is when we intentionally schedule mindfulness into our daily lives. We plan ahead to take time throughout our day to engage in some sort of mindfulness activity. This can include a morning breathing exercise or body scan, taking breaks to go for a mindfulness walk or just scheduling reminders to pause and check in with yourself in a mindful way.

2. **In-the-moment mindfulness:** This is when we implement a mindfulness exercise in response to some stressful or emotional situation. This can include pausing to take a deep breath in response to a stressor, closing your eyes and paying attention to your body during a panicky moment or just noticing muscle tension you might be experiencing during a tense conversation.

Some Mindfulness Strategies

Regardless of whether you are trying to include mindfulness as a planned or an in-the-moment strategy, there are particular approaches that will make it most effective for you.

- **Start simple:** You don't need to start with a 20-minute mindfulness routine. Taking brief moments throughout the day – even taking one, deep, slow breath and paying attention to how it feels – can be an effective way to start.

- **Don't worry about clearing your mind:** Despite popular conceptions, mindfulness isn't about clearing your mind of all thoughts, it's about noticing your thoughts as they happen. Try to simply let those thoughts occur and pay attention to them as they happen.[9]

---

[9] This is where I get hung up. I let my mind go, realize I haven't been paying attention and get frustrated with myself. I need to get better at the part where I just bring myself back to my breath without the frustration.

- **Engage with your senses:** As with grounding (Hack 37), it's helpful to focus on your senses. In fact, picking one sense and paying attention to it for a short time can be a good way to try mindfulness.
- **Be patient with yourself:**[10] Do what you can to be kind and patient with yourself as you try this hack. There will be times when you let your mind wander and you get distracted. Try to accept that as part of the experience as it will be a much more valuable process if you aren't criticizing yourself while you do it.
- **Consider a guided app:** There are a variety of guided apps that can be helpful in encouraging mindfulness. Typically, the apps provide a narrative for you to listen to as you follow a step-by step process to focus on the here and now.

These approaches can be helpful both with planned mindfulness or when you're struggling through a particularly challenging and stressful moment. Taking time to pay attention to the present moment will often leave you feeling reset and ready to move on in a healthy way.

[10]   OK, so this is also where I get hung up ... I'll work on it.

Hack 43: Take a Broader View

Self-Immersed vs. Self-Distanced

Take a moment to think of a time when you were really angry or really sad. Now, visualize that event as if you're a third party nearby, watching and witnessing what's going on. Try to evaluate what happened, including why you felt the way you did, from that observer's perspective. What would that person say about what you're feeling and why you're feeling it? (The *why* is especially important here.)

This is one way of self-distancing for emotion regulation. It's a strategy you can use to better understand the emotions you're feeling in a way that helps you manage them. A 2005 study explored this exact approach by asking participants to recall a negative emotional event from their life and then placing them into one of two experimental groups: (1) self-immersed, where they relived the experience through their own eyes and (2) self-distanced, where they imagined it as an observer would.[xxxvii] The researchers then assessed the participants' emotional reactivity, level of insight regarding the event, whether they felt it had been resolved, etc.

The researchers found that the distanced group was less angry, had lower scores on a test of other negative emotions, interpreted the event in a healthier way and was less likely to ruminate. Years later, in a 2011 paper, two of the same authors reviewed a number of research studies on this same topic and found that self-distancing led to healthier interpretations of emotions, less rumination, less emotional distress and less physiological activation.[xxxviii]

How to Distance Yourself

There are a variety of ways to take a broader view of a situation.

Of course, you can imagine being a third-party observer as was done in the research above. But you can also think about it from a temporal perspective by asking yourself, "How will I feel about this in a week or a month or a year?" You can think about what advice you might give to a friend who was going through this situation or imagine how you would write about it in your memoir at the end of your life. You can even take a moment to talk about yourself in the third person, as a way of providing some additional distance from the situation.[11]

A key point here is that you're not trying to avoid or minimize the emotion. You're trying to create some distance between you and the feeling so that you can take a broader perspective and develop a more nuanced understanding. For example, imagine that you're really anxious about an upcoming event or task. Your immediate reaction might be something like, "I'm going to mess this up." To take a distancing approach you can ask yourself, "What would I tell a friend who was going through this?" or "If I do screw it up, will it still matter one year from now?" These subtle reframes allow you to think differently about both the situation and the emotions emerging from it.

Asking Why

One element that is critical here is to evaluate *why*.[12]

[11]   Ryan feels weird asking you to talk about yourself in the third person, but Ryan's going to do it anyway because he thinks it might be helpful to you.

[12]   It's funny because as a therapist, I was actually discouraged from asking "why questions" because they might sound judgmental. Saying "Why did you feel like that?" might make someone feel judged in a way that saying "What made you feel like that?" wouldn't. I honestly think this is silly. Even if it is true that why questions make people feel defensive and judged, that's something you can talk about in the session. "I ask why questions because sometimes I want to know why. If that ever makes you feel judged or defensive, let's talk about it."

Remember, emotions are a source of information. They tell you something about your circumstances or about yourself. As I discussed with Hacks 35 and 36, part of the goal here is to listen to what an emotion is telling you, and that requires asking yourself why. The other thing about asking yourself why is that it shifts you from a place of emotionality to a place of inquiry and questioning. By focusing less on the feeling itself and instead interrogating whatever is happening beneath the feeling, you both minimize the intensity of the negative feeling and develop a broader and healthier understanding of your feelings more generally.

Hack 44: Avoid Exercise and Catharsis

Blind Threading Nickel-Sized Discs

In 1972, three researchers published an article in the *Journal of Experimental Social Psychology*, in which they described a concept called "excitation transfer."[xxxix] They had 38 participants come to a lab where they were told they would be involved in two studies, one on learning and a second on exercise. However, this was a lie.[13] It was just one study with two parts.

The first part of the study involved the participants sharing their opinions with someone they thought was another participant in a different room (but who was actually a researcher involved in the study).[14] In response to these opinions, either a light flashed on to signal the supposed other participant's agreement or the participants received a mild electric shock to express disagreement. While they were told this study was on the impact of punishment on learning, the entire point of this first step was to make them angry. There were two groups of participants, a group that received three mild shocks (the not-that-angry group) and a group that received nine more intense shocks (the much angrier group).

After this was over, participants from both groups engaged in one of two different tasks. They either rode an exercise bike for a few minutes or engaged in "the continuous 'blind' threading of nickel-sized discs with off-center holes" for the equivalent amount of time. In other words, one of these tasks was designed to increase physiological arousal (equivalent to exercise) and the other was intentionally boring. When the

---

[13]   It really feels like almost all psychological research from the 1960s and 1970s involved lying to participants.

[14]   See! More LIES!

participants were done with this task, they were given the opportunity to administer shocks back to the person who had shocked them.

The researchers found that the group that exercised was significantly more aggressive than the group who had engaged in the boring task, showing that exercise doesn't have the cathartic anger-reducing quality that people think it does. In fact, in this study it had the opposite impact. Not only was the exercise group still angry, they were angrier than they would have been if they had done something different.

Excitation Transfer and Catharsis

Here's what's happening. When you're emotional, you're in a state of elevated physiological arousal. Your heart rate increases, your muscles are tense, etc. If your goal is to decrease that feeling state, you need to decrease the physiological arousal. Vigorous exercise does the opposite of that. It increases that arousal, and so it has the effect of intensifying the emotional experience. This is referred to as "excitation transfer," when arousal from one activity intensifies emotional feelings not directly related to it.[15]

This is ultimately why deep breathing, mindfulness and grounding are so valuable in these emotional moments. When the goal is to decrease arousal, these three approaches have that effect. They de-escalate the physiological intensity associated with the emotion in a way that limits the potential for excitation transfer.

A variation of this is what's referred to as catharsis – attempts to "vent" negative-feeling emotions, especially anger, through aggression by using a punching bag or

---

[15] This is the origin of the manipulative dating tactic of doing something scary on a first date (e.g., amusement park, motorcycle ride, scary movie). The theory, and some research would suggest that it works, is that the arousal from the activity will be interpreted as feelings of attraction.

breaking things. Here we see a similar set of findings as with exercise. Decades' worth of research has shown us that this sort of catharsis increases anger and other negative emotions. A 2024 meta-analysis that reviewed 154 different published articles on anger-management approaches found that punching and breaking things didn't reduce anger, and sometimes even increased it.[xl] Despite being incredibly popular, these approaches simply don't work and should be avoided.

Two Important Caveats

All that said, there are two important caveats. The first is that maybe your goal isn't to decrease the arousal or the emotion. If you're in a situation where you think that anger, sadness, fear, etc. will serve you somehow (athletics is a common example, with many athletes saying that they perform better when they are angry), you may not want to embrace an emotion-reduction strategy. In that case, excitation transfer may work for you.

The second caveat is that there are some forms of exercise – those that don't increase arousal – which might still be helpful. For example, some types of yoga might involve less arousal and serve the important purpose of helping you focus and ground your mindfulness. Similarly, going for a walk (especially in nature), in a way that keeps arousal low, might be an effective way to get active while also helping de-escalate the emotional intensity.

CHAPTER 8
EMOTIONAL EXPRESSION HACKS

Of course, as we feel the emotion, we often act on it. Emotions aren't just internal experiences, they shape our behavior. Sometimes that means slamming a door, raising our voice or crying. Other times it's more subtle: a shift in tone, a cold shoulder or avoiding someone or something. These emotional expressions are powerful and important because they communicate what we're feeling to the people around us.

In this chapter, I'll explore strategies for managing emotional expression. This isn't about suppressing emotions or pretending everything is fine. It's about learning to express feelings in ways that reflect your values and goals, rather than reacting automatically. Whether it's slowing down a heated reaction or learning how to share what you're feeling more clearly, these tools can help you respond with purpose instead of impulsivity. Specifically, you'll learn to express your feelings productively using the following hacks.

- Hack 45: Write About It
- Hack 46: Communicate Assertively
- Hack 47: Practice Problem Solving
- Hack 48: Channel Emotion into Creativity
- Hack 49: Seek Social Support
- Hack 50: Seek Broader Change

Emotional expressions are a natural and important part of how we respond to what we're feeling, but they're also something we can shape and hone. These next hacks will help you express yourself in ways that are thoughtful, effective and aligned with who you want to be.

Hack 45: Write About It

Attending to Your Own Story Arc

One of my favorite things to do after finishing watching a TV show is to sit down and talk with others who have watched it. More specifically, I like to talk about the story arcs of the different characters. What were these characters like, what motivated them and how did they change over the course of the show? The more nuanced the characters are – especially from an emotional perspective – the more I enjoy the conversation.

Of course, we can and should do this with our own lives too. We can dig into our own story arcs to better understand our motivations and how we're changing as a result of our experiences. And writing might be a really valuable way to do exactly this. In fact, in 2014 a team of researchers studied this exact question. Can writing improve mood by helping people better understand themselves and their feelings?[xli] The researchers carried out an experiment in which they assigned 113 adults to either an expressive writing group or a controlled writing group. In the latter, participants wrote about their daily activities in a neutral way, with no emotions and no judgment. For 4 sessions of 20 minutes each, participants were given writing prompts (e.g., "What did you do yesterday?," "What will you do when you're done writing?") and they were told explicitly, "I am not interested in your emotions or opinions."

Meanwhile, in the expressive writing group, participants were told to write for 20 minutes on their "deepest feelings and thoughts" about a stressful experience they have had. They were given instructions to tie the experience to other parts of their life, even to consider how the experience related to their childhood. The results here – along with other findings on expressive writing – are a little more complicated than they have been with other emotion hacks. In this case, some participants benefited. Specifically, those who were high on "emotional expressivity" already (i.e., those who were already comfortable sharing their emotions). Those who weren't already emotionally expressive actually felt worse after doing expressive writing.

Other research has found that in the short term, writing about emotional events often increases distress and negative mood, but has long-term benefits connected to emotional and social wellbeing.[xlii] There have even been some physical health benefits identified, such as reduced blood pressure, improved immune system functioning and fewer visits to the doctor. Collectively, what you can take from these findings is that the benefits are not universal and that writing can actually be counterproductive for some people.

Mileage May Vary

These mixed results make a lot of sense when you think about them. First, of course people who are writing about a trauma or other highly emotional event might feel worse immediately after writing. They've just spent 20 minutes elaborating on what was by definition a deeply upsetting event. Much like how people react to therapy, you would expect some immediate distress even when there are long-term benefits.

Second, some people might be more ready to engage with this exercise than others. The research suggests that expressive writing is most valuable for people who are already emotionally expressive, who feel ready to process these emotional experiences and who are open to emotional vulnerability. For people who are already used to identifying and articulating emotions, writing about them feels much more natural and aligns with their already-present coping style. They are open to some level of emotional vulnerability and willing to reflect on difficult events. This puts them in an emotionally healthier place to start the exercise and so they are more likely to experience the benefits of writing as a way of understanding themselves.

Third, expressive writing is probably unhelpful or even harmful to people who struggle with emotional expressivity or are highly avoidant of emotions. For people who find it hard to articulate their feelings in a meaningful way or for whom opening up emotionally is painful, expressive writing may end up exacerbating negative feelings or lead to additional discomfort or frustration.

To sum up, much like analyzing the story arcs of characters in a TV show, expressive writing can help people better understand their emotional experiences. But its effectiveness depends heavily on the individual. Whether or not you embrace expressive writing is linked to how comfortable you already are with expressing emotions. For those who are comfortable, it can lead to improved mood, greater personal insight and even some physical health benefits.

Hack 46: Communicate Assertively

An Important Thing That's Hard to Do Well

Any conversation about emotional wellness should include discussion of assertive communication. I consider it a necessary aspect of healthy emotion management, and the research bears this out. Assertiveness is associated with improved emotion regulation, reduced stress, increased emotional intelligence, decreased likelihood of burnout and overall mental wellness. Learning to assert yourself will decrease your tendency to suppress emotions, allowing you to express negative emotions in a way that is less likely to damage relationships. It will also improve your confidence, especially during times of conflict.

The only problem with assertiveness is that it's hard to do well. By definition, it requires you to stand up for yourself while also considering the rights and viewpoints of the other people involved. That means you need to be able to understand complicated emotional situations from a variety of perspectives. You have to be able to think reasonably about what you and the others involved in a situation deserve, and to be able to communicate all of that in a clear, direct and respectful way.

Let's break down three broad types of communication: assertive, passive and aggressive. Assertive communication expresses your thoughts and feelings in a direct, honest and respectful way. You're working to communicate your wants without violating the rights of others. Passive communication prioritizes the avoidance of conflict, so you might use more vague or indirect language. You sacrifice your own wants – or even rights – for the benefit of others. Finally, aggressive communication expresses your thoughts and feelings in a way that's disrespectful or harmful to others. You prioritize your own needs and wants, disregarding the boundaries or rights of others.

Why Assertiveness Training Helps

There was a time when assertiveness training was a critical aspect of many therapeutic interventions, but as Dr. Brittany Speed and colleagues point out in a 2018 article – "Assertiveness Training: A Forgotten Evidence-Based Practice" – such training has become an underutilized approach.[xliii] They argue that it's useful for treating a host of psychological issues, including relationship problems, workplace stress, burnout and low self-esteem. Specifically, they highlight its value in the treatment of anxiety and depressive disorders, pointing out that many people struggling with those conditions suffer from social skills deficits that exacerbate the problems. Such people avoid conflict and fail to set boundaries in a way that makes their emotional challenges more severe.

Ultimately, assertiveness training is important for two reasons. First, assertiveness deficits have emotional consequences. When you suppress your own wants and needs in favor of conflict avoidance, you often end up feeling resentful and frustrated. You may also feel guilty for allowing others to take advantage of you. These thoughts and feelings might take a long-term emotional toll on you. The second reason assertiveness training is important is because it often leads directly to healthy emotion regulation. When you can express your feelings in a healthy way, you decrease the tendency to suppress your emotions, learn to decrease conflict and also increase your tolerance for emotional discomfort.

Learning to Assert Yourself

Of course, as I said earlier, self-assertiveness is difficult. It's a skill that requires knowledge, practice and effort. Here are some strategies you can embrace to learn to do it well.

- **Understand your rights:** A critical part of assertiveness is knowing what you have a right to (and knowing what you don't have a right to). Appropriate assertiveness means that you understand the difference between something you deserve and something you just really want.
- **Use "I statements":** Try to focus your part of the conversation on your own experiences by saying things like "I feel" or "I'd prefer." This type of language helps limit the potential for blame.
- **Get used to sitting in discomfort:** As I wrote in Hack 41, Embrace Emotional Discomfort, you sometimes need to lean into uncomfortable feelings. Assertive conversations will likely be emotionally uncomfortable, especially if you've been suppressing your feelings for a long time. Learning to be assertive means learning to be OK with such discomfort.
- **Stay calm:** This is a place where your tone matters. If you come across as loud or overly emotional, you run the risk of being perceived as aggressive rather than assertive. The goal should be to present your thoughts and feelings in a way in which both you and the other person feel respected – and that requires a level of composure.
- **Plan ahead:** Chances are, you can already think of some circumstances (either types of situations or specific people) where you tend to give in. If you can identify such circumstances, you can plan for them and even practice ahead of time. You can tell yourself, "I tend to give in to this person, so this time I'm going to say … "

Approaches such as these help form the foundation of healthy, respectful communication that protects your emotional wellbeing and potentially strengthens your relationships. By embracing them, you build the confidence to speak up even when uncomfortable.

Hack 47: Practice Problem Solving

When Emotions Signal a Problem

One of the most important ideas I've tried to convey in this book is that we need to pay attention to the information our emotions provide. In Hacks 35 and 36, I wrote that you need to listen to what your emotions tell you about the situation you're in and what they tell you about yourself. Taken together, one of the things your emotions are probably alerting you to is the presence of a problem in your life. One way to regulate your emotions, then, is to channel the energy those feelings provide into a solution to that problem.

This isn't a terribly novel idea in the sense that you've probably done versions of this throughout your entire life. Some regular frustration (e.g., your printer not printing correctly, frequent traffic) has no doubt motivated you to solve the problem (get a new printer, identify a new route to work). What I'm encouraging you to do is to be more intentional about it as an emotion-management strategy. When you're feeling something intensely, stop and ask yourself what problem might be causing it, and consider what you might be able to do to address that problem.

What Is Problem Solving?

Problem solving is the process of identifying a challenge, generating a list of possible solutions, evaluating each of the options and then implementing one of them to address the original problem. While it's a cognitive process that exists to address life challenges, it has a significant impact on your emotional life too. First, and this one is obvious, finding solutions to reoccurring problems makes it less likely you'll face these problems in the future. For example, when you identify a new route to work, you're less likely to run into frustration-inducing traffic.

Second, and more importantly, problem solving moves you from feeling stuck and helpless to a place of empowerment. It's action-oriented so the steps you're taking to address the challenge often feel good in a way that undoes the negative feelings you were having. For example, imagine the anxiety you feel when you have an overwhelming to-do list. For many, this situation leads to avoidance. They spiral about how much there is to do and instead of working through it, they become paralyzed with anxiety. They might try to distract themselves by watching TV or scrolling through social media, all the while this overwhelming to-do list is weighing heavily on them.

A problem-solving approach would include someone stepping back and mapping out a plan to get all the things on their list done. They would make a list, estimating how long they think each item will take, and they schedule when they'll do those things in a way that allows them to meet any deadlines they have. If they find that some of those items are impossible or unrealistic to accomplish, they come up with alternative plans even if those include communicating to someone that they can't meet a deadline and need an extension. In doing so, the person eliminates the unknowns and starts to feel less anxious, not because they've done all the work but because they have a realistic plan for how the work will get done.

How to Manage Your Emotions through Problem Solving

So, we know it's valuable and can feel empowering, but how do you use problem solving productively? Here are five steps for implementing a solution-focused approach to emotion management.

1. **Identify the problem:** The first step is to work out what's leading to your negative feelings. To do that, identify what is happening that has you feeling anxious, angry, sad, etc. For example, imagine the problem is that you feel anxious about your romantic partner pulling away from you.

2. **Identify the parts you can control:** In any situation, there are parts you can control and/or influence, and there are parts you can't. Take time to identify the elements of the situation that are outside your control and which parts you can change. For example, while you can't control your partner's feelings, you can control how you communicate with them and how you manage your thoughts about the situation.

3. **Generate possible solutions:** Based on what you can and can't control, identify three or four possible solutions. They don't have to be perfect and it's probably better not to worry yet about the best thing to do. Just come up with ideas. So, if you're worried about your partner pulling away, some solutions might be to share those concerns with them or to focus on your own wellbeing if the relationship should end.

4. **Select one solution and start:** Once you've generated some possible solutions, pick the most realistic and try it. The process of starting something will alleviate at least some of the emotional discomfort. For example, you could decide to communicate your concerns to your partner in an open and honest way, and then make decisions about how to have that conversation.

5. **Reassess and make changes:** Finally, whatever decision you made can be re-evaluated at any point. If you find it's not working the way you wanted it to or you're still struggling emotionally, take a moment to think through alternatives and adjust (again bearing in mind which parts you can control). If the conversation with your partner goes poorly, and you feel them pulling away even more, you can shift to another direction and focus on your own

wellbeing. At least now, you know where things stand and you aren't feeling stuck the way you were.

An important thing to remember is that problem solving doesn't guarantee a perfect outcome. There's no promise that you'll get exactly what you want from this. But, by shifting from spiraling thoughts to some sort of intentional action, you'll likely reclaim a sense of control and that might bring some emotional relief.

Hack 48: Channel Emotion into Creativity

Articulating Your Feelings

I was doing an interview for a podcast once where I tried to describe ways you can channel your anger into creativity. The host blurted out at one point, "Look, if I'm angry I'm not going to sit down and write a poem about it." And he's right, he probably wouldn't. Honestly, I probably wouldn't either. Creative writing or art is not my go-to approach for channeling emotions. But I know people who do use it. In fact, I work with a number of people and have taught quite a few students who might sit down and write a poem or a short story, or create music, or knit, draw, paint or do any of a number of different artistic endeavors as a way of channeling their emotions.

Now I know we talked about engaging in the arts earlier in Hack 15, but that was different to what we're talking about here. Hack 15 was about how attending art workshops or going to concerts can help stave off unwanted emotions. It was about the importance of building art into your life (much like how eating healthily, spending time in nature or staying physically fit can also prevent you from experiencing unhealthy emotions). Here, what I'm saying is that when you *are* experiencing a strong emotion, you can channel it into creative acts as a way of processing or managing those emotions.

There are actually entire sub-disciplines dedicated to art therapies. These are essentially approaches to mental health treatment that use the arts (defined broadly to include visual and performing arts such as dance, music, painting, drama, etc.) to help people explore and express their emotions, resolve inner conflicts and improve their overall wellbeing. These activities aren't so much about artistic skill, where the goal is to share the work (though, that certainly can happen).

They are about processing emotions and developing insight through the act of artistic creation and creative expression.

The idea is that some people have a difficult time articulating their emotions verbally and the arts provide a mechanism through which they can express their feelings without needing to come up with the exact words to describe them. Instead of trying to get a client to translate emotional experiences into words, they can share those feelings through a painting, dance or music.

The Value of Art Therapy

In 2014, four researchers reviewed the published research on the therapeutic use of dance, looking at 23 different articles from the 20 years prior.[xliv] They found that across studies, dance movement therapy was effective in decreasing symptoms of depression and anxiety and in improving overall quality of life. Similar findings have been made for music therapy and visual art therapy.

The Self-Expression and Emotion Regulation in Art Therapy Scale measures the perceived benefits of art therapy.[xlv] Typically, clients report that creating art helps them express their emotions, particularly those that are difficult for them to express ("Art therapy helps me express things I can't put into words"[xlvi]), and also helps them regulate their emotions. They report that art therapy allows them to decrease emotional intensity when they're feeling overwhelmed (e.g., "making art helps me calm down"[xlvii]) and increase general emotional awareness (e.g., "through art therapy, I better understand my feelings"[xlviii]). In other words, art provided people with a valuable mechanism to channel their anger, sadness, fear or guilt into something creative.

How to Channel Your Emotions into Art

If you want to try this hack, you need to know a few things. There's no right or wrong way to go about channeling your emotions into creativity. The goal isn't to make something beautiful (though you may end up making something beautiful in the process); it's to better understand and use your emotions. Here are some suggestions to get you started.

- **Start with the feeling:** Before you do anything, pause and ask yourself what you're feeling and then let that emotion guide what you create. Try to remember that it doesn't need to be logical and it doesn't need to speak to anyone but you.
- **Use prompts if you feel stuck:** It might feel intimidating to start from nothing, so consider using some prompts to kick yourself off (e.g., draw your anxiety, make a visual map of your anger). Such prompts will give you a starting place that you can move forward from.[1]
- **Don't feel the need to reflect but know that you can if you want:** This process of creativity will be effective even if you don't analyze what you made or try to take meaning from it. But if it feels OK, take a few moments after you have finished to pay attention to the art and see if anything in you shifted emotionally as a result.
- **Don't feel the need to share:** Remember that what you created was for you. You can keep it, share it publicly or tear it up and throw it away. Or you can choose to show it to just a few people you trust. The goal was to express your feelings, so do whatever helps you to do that.

---

[1]   I do this a lot when I journal. I have a list of prompts ranging from "Write about your last dream" to "Create a story inspired by a childhood memory." They give me something to start with when I'm feeling a little stuck and need new ideas.

Channeling your emotions into art isn't about making something beautiful; it's about making space for what you feel. Whether you write, paint, dance or simply make something for yourself, the act of creating can help you express what's hard to say, and regulate what feels overwhelming.

Hack 49: Seek Social Support

The Buffering Effects of Social Support

There's a famous psychological paper from 1985 that studies how social support influences emotional wellbeing.[xlix] It's a review of approximately 40 studies that explore the relationship between stress, social support and psychological and physical health. While it had long been known that social support – the experience of having others who care for you and are willing and able to help you – impacts your emotions positively, how it did so was somewhat unclear. What the authors found was that social support provided what they called a "buffering effect" – protection against the negative impacts of stress on our emotional lives.

The article talks about social support in two different ways: structural and functional. Structural support can be thought of largely in terms of quantity. Do you have social relationships? How many family members and friends do you have? Are you partnered? Do you live alone? How often do you socialize? Do you engage in some sort of community group (e.g., religious organization, clubs)? Structural support matters. The more socially connected you are, the better your emotional health. But what the article found was that structural support doesn't matter as much as functional support.

Functional support refers to getting specific types of help through your relationships. For example, do you have people you can go to for guidance and advice (e.g., legal or medical expertise)? Do you have people you can count on for help when you need it (e.g., rides when your car breaks down, childcare when a sitter falls through)? Do you have people you can go to for emotional support, empathy or just to distract you when you're feeling down? These types of supports have an insulating effect in that they protect you from stress when you experience negative events.

A Trusted Person You Can Go To

For example, take someone whose spouse passes away. Over the next few weeks and months, ignoring for now the emotional toll such a loss will take, they will have a variety of legal and practical situations to navigate (e.g., planning a funeral service, addressing a new financial reality, etc.). Those things are overwhelming under any circumstances, but they are made less overwhelming when you have supports to rely on: a friend you can go to for advice, people to bring you food, someone to watch your kids or to help you move if necessary. Those sources of support don't eliminate the pain of the loss, but they do lesson the emotional consequences of the loss.

Above and beyond that, having a trusted person you can go to for your emotional needs in those moments also serves to provide that buffering effect. Having someone who will listen to you and care for you without judgment will ease that emotional suffering. They might help you feel less alone and make it easier for you to process what you're going through. In fact, even just *believing* you have people you can go to can provide that buffering effect.

Developing and Using Social Support

To effectively seek social support for emotion management, you need to do two things: (1) build a social support network and (2) be willing and able to reach out to that network when you need it. Both these things require some intentionality, effort and skill. Starting with building a social support network, there are three things you should do.

1. **Expand and diversify that network:** Try to build connections across different areas of your life so you have a variety of people to turn to for different types of support.

2. **Connect regularly:** Do what you can to stay in touch through regular check-ins to keep the relationships strong.
3. **Foster mutual support:** Do what you can to be there for others too. Relationships operate best when they don't feel one-sided.

In terms of reaching out to that network in times of distress, be intentional about taking these five steps.

1. **Connect with the right person:** Different situations might call for different responses. Try to reach out to someone you can trust, who has shown empathy and trustworthiness in the past.
2. **Tell the person honestly what you need:** Be clear with them regarding what you might need. Do you want advice, support and empathy, or just someone to listen?
3. **Share what you feel comfortable sharing, including the feelings themselves:** Try to open up as much as you feel you can, allowing your feelings to be seen without feeling embarrassment or shame. Do what feels comfortable, though still challenge yourself to step outside that comfort zone within reason.
4. **Let the person help you:** Try not to push your suffering away or to downplay how you're feeling. If they offer you something that you think will be helpful, accept that support from them.
5. **Show appreciation:** Be intentional about showing your gratitude as it will strengthen the relationship moving forward.

An additional benefit to seeking out social support in this way is that it fosters stronger relationships in the future. Meaningful friendships are often built not just on shared experiences but through moments of vulnerability. When one person opens up to another and learns that they can trust the person, it paves the way for more such connections.

Hack 50: Seek Broader Change

Fueling You to Confront Injustice

People use a lot of different metaphors to describe emotion. We sometimes embrace a pressure-based metaphor, comparing ourselves to pressure cookers or talking about how we're keeping things bottled up or it being time to blow off steam. Other times we talk about emotions as though they are the weather, referring to sunny dispositions, clouded judgment, emotional fogs or stormy periods. Or, perhaps we liken our feelings to physical sensations, describing emotional experiences as heartache, gut feelings or lumps in our throats.

My preferred emotion metaphor, though, is to think of our feelings as fuel. You hear this one in descriptions of rage igniting conflict or adding fuel to a fire. We sometimes refer to situations as being emotionally charged but also talk about being burned out or running on empty and needing to recharge. All of this speaks to something fundamental about our feelings – anger, sadness, fear, grief, love, curiosity, all of them – they are not passive. They are sources of energy and power. They drive action and decision making. They fuel you to do things you might not otherwise do. And it is because they are fuel that you can use them to seek broader change.

The central message of my TED talk, "Why We Get Mad", was that your anger exists because it alerts you to injustice and then fuels you to confront that injustice. When you get mad and your sympathetic nervous system activates (i.e., when your heart starts racing, your muscles tense up and you start to sweat), it's one of the ways your body prepares you to respond to cruelty. But this is ultimately true of all emotions. Your fear alerts you to danger and your sadness alerts you to loss. Your disgust alerts you to contamination, your shame and embarrassment alert you to having made a mistake, and your jealousy alerts you to an unmet desire.

Then, the arousal that accompanies these feelings acts as fuel to give you the energy you need to act. You can channel that energy into broader, systemic change that's focused on whatever led to the emotion in the first place. We don't have to look very hard to see cases where collective anger led to social change. I would argue that most, if not all, social movements start that way. There's an anger-inducing spark that leads to action.

Yet there's actually some research on this that reveals that we need more, emotionally-speaking, than just the spark. In 2004, researchers looked at the emotions that predicted collective action.[1] Using a very clever method, they designed a study to explore how students would respond to tuition fee increases, but they manipulated the participants' understanding of (1) whether the increase impacted them or other students and (2) whether their peers were similarly outraged and ready to take action. The researchers found that the best predictor of action was when students were angry *and* believed that they and their peers could make a difference.

Powerful Emotions Can Get You Started

What the above tells us more than anything is that we should think of our emotions as having two overlapping roles in creating systemic change. First, powerful emotions such as anger, grief or fear can get you started. These emotions can provide a spark because they essentially communicate to you that something is very wrong and that you need to act. They draw your attention to the problem, provide direction, signal that you need to do something and give you the initial energy to get started.

Second, emotions play a role in sustaining the action. The spark from that initial emotion might burn out without additional fuel to keep it going. More anger, grief and fear might help here, but eventually people need some more positive-feeling emotions such as hope, pride and solidarity. Like that 2004 study, people need to believe that change will come, that others are working on it too and that those others have their backs. They need to feel good about what they're working on and believe they're making progress.

How to Channel Emotions into Change

Based on all of the above, I would argue that there are three steps you need to take to effectively channel your emotions into broader change.

1. **Before you act, you need to figure out where you want to go.** The fuel provides the energy, but you need to be strategic about how to move forward in an intentional way. Emotions give you the power to move, but without a clear direction you're spinning your wheels. Before you act, ask yourself, "What's my goal, where am I going and how do I get there intentionally?"
2. **Then, be cognizant of the emotions that will sustain that movement.** Negative-feeling emotions likely initiated the effort, but what emotions will keep it going? More importantly, can you be intentional about harnessing those emotions to maintain the energy? Those emotions that sparked the action – such as anger, fear or sadness – won't always be the ones to carry you forward. To sustain that momentum, you need to be intentional about cultivating other feelings such as hope and solidarity.
3. **Remember that like any fuel, our emotions are volatile.** They can be reactive, unstable and, if we don't handle them with caution, may combust. Strong emotions are unpredictable. If you don't take time to process and manage them effectively, they can lead to impulsive decisions or actions that undermine your goals.

Remember, your emotions are not obstacles to overcome. They are signals, catalysts and power sources. When you understand how to channel them, they start working for you. With direction, awareness and care, your feelings can become one of the most effective tools you have for creating real and lasting change.

Final Thoughts

Extraordinarily Stressful Times

It's undeniable that we are living in extraordinarily stressful times right now. We've just gotten through an international health crisis that took the lives of over 7 million people globally. There's significant political unrest in the United States and in the world more broadly. Related to this, there's considerable global economic uncertainty that's leading to both practical and emotional consequences. Add to that the technological developments that, while amazing, also threaten to change so much of what we do and how we do it.

For me, personally, the last few years have been the most stressful time of my life. Just a few weeks after I signed the book contract to write *Emotion Hacks*, I was offered a new job as Dean of the College of Arts, Humanities, and Social Sciences at the University of Wisconsin–Green Bay, the same university where I had worked for the previous 18 years. I truly love this job. I'm surrounded by great people at a university that is thriving and I find the work exceedingly rewarding. But it's very different to what I was doing before and there was a steep learning curve. Plus, there are a lot of people counting on me, so taken together, it's a stressful brew.[2]

What We Can and Cannot Control

What I'm getting at above is that the world is full of shared and personal stressors. The global challenges I mentioned impact all of us, but in different ways. For some, the economic uncertainty is personal. Their financial livelihood

---

[2]   Please don't think any of this is a complaint. Compared to most people, my life is exceedingly easy and I'm thankful for all of the opportunities I have.

is challenged and their ability to use the hacks described in this book is affected. For others, that economic uncertainty is less direct, but the political unrest has them living in a near constant state of anxiety.

These are things that exist largely outside our control. I can't change the political climate no matter how much I want to. I can't undo what clearly will be a seismic shift in education as a result of generative artificial intelligence. These are things that, by and large, we just accept as part of our reality right now that we must live with.

However, I do get to decide – at least partially – *how* I live with those things. How do I choose to engage with this new technology? What do I encourage my faculty, staff and students to do with it? How do I engage with politics? When and what do I protest? When do I turn on the news and when do I tune it out? How do I take care of myself and how do I help my family take care of themselves? How can I find time for healthy sleep, healthy exercise and healthy eating at a time when so much feels extraordinarily scary and overwhelming?

That's Where the Emotion Hacks Come In

This book is about finding the subtle life shifts we can make to change our emotional experiences in a positive way, so that even when the big things are scary or frustrating or overwhelming, we're taking care of the little things. We make decisions about the stressors we invite into our lives. We make decisions about how we take care of ourselves so that when we face unexpected stressors, we are better able to deal with them. We pay attention to the thoughts we're having and we actively try to change those thoughts when we realize they are causing us problems. We let ourselves feel our feelings and we listen to those feelings so we that can make intentional decisions about whether we try to calm ourselves down or channel those emotions into something productive.

I'll be transparent with you and tell you that there were times over the last two years when this book started to feel like a list of things I wasn't doing very well. Getting healthy sleep? Nope. Eating well? Not really. Socializing? Not unless you count work meetings. I actually started to feel like a bit of hypocrite. Who was I to tell people they should take all these preventative measures to manage their emotions when I wasn't even doing some of these basics? And then I remembered two things. First, nobody's perfect. Second, this book was never supposed to be a list of things everyone must do.

As for the first point – nobody's perfect – I've always believed myself to be a work in progress. I've always wanted to work toward trying to be a little bit better each day, and I've always known that improvement isn't linear. It's OK I've had a little slip this last year, provided I'm intentional about trying to improve. I can give myself grace and try to do better.

With the second point – that this book was never supposed to be a list of 50 things everyone must do – it was easy to forget that while I was writing it. It was easy to get hung up on the things I wasn't doing. I hope that didn't happen to you while you were reading it. I hope you were able to remember that the goal here is to better understand emotions generally, to get a feel for the subtle life changes that will help you have a healthier emotional life, and to pick the ones that work best for you right now. I hope this book continues to be a resource even now that you've finished it, and that you can revisit those things you're not yet doing so that you too can give yourself grace and continue to try to work on yourself when you need to.

ACKNOWLEDGEMENTS

Once again, I find myself profoundly grateful to the many people who helped bring this book to life. Whether through encouragement, insight, collaboration or simply showing up when I needed it, their support made this work possible.

First and foremost, I owe an enormous debt to my family. Their love, patience and humor are woven into everything I do. The emotional grounding they offer provides the stability I need to take creative risks and explore difficult topics like this with honesty and nuance. I am especially grateful for the way they listen, challenge and cheer me on – all while navigating the everyday complexities of life. This book, like the two before it, is better because I am surrounded by people who believe in me. They are my most consistent reminder of why emotional wellness matters.

I'm also incredibly fortunate to have an extended network of friends and loved ones whose presence is both comforting and energizing. They ask the right questions, send quick messages of support or congratulations, or make me laugh when I need it most. Professionally, I've had the privilege of working in a space filled with curiosity and creativity. At University of Wisconsin - Green Bay, I'm surrounded by smart and compassionate people – faculty, staff and students – who model what it means to think deeply and care genuinely. I benefit daily from their insight and energy, and I draw inspiration from the intellectual community we're building together.

One of the most unexpectedly powerful parts of the last few years has been connecting with people through social media. When I first began sharing ideas online, I had no idea it would become such a meaningful space for me to both share my thoughts and learn from others. Thousands of people have shared their stories with me. These conversations have made my work more honest, more grounded and more attuned to what people are really going through. If you've ever messaged me, commented on a post or just taken in something I've shared - thank you. You've contributed to this book in ways you may not even realize.

I am, as always, thankful for the team at Watkins. Their editorial support, thoughtful guidance and deep understanding of this project have made the process smoother and the product stronger. They've shown tremendous patience and faith in me, especially when ideas took longer to develop than expected. It is wonderful to work with people who not only believe in the message but also help you deliver it with clarity and impact.

Finally, I remain deeply indebted to the researchers and practitioners who have dedicated their lives to understanding emotion – especially those who focus on anger. Their work laid the foundation for this book and continues to shape the way I think, teach and write.

ENDNOTES

i   Gross, J.J. (2002). Emotion regulation: Affective, cognitive and social consequences. *Psychophysiology, 39*(3), 281–91.

ii   Dubad, M., Elahi, F. & Marwaha, S. (2021). The clinical impacts of mobile mood-monitoring in young people with mental health problems: The MeMO study. *Frontiers in Psychiatry, 12,* 687270.

iii   Van Bockstaele, B., Atticciati, L., Hiekkaranta, A.P., Larsen, H. & Verschuere, B. (2020). Choose change: Situation modification, distraction and reappraisal in mild versus intense negative situations. *Motivation and Emotion, 44*(4), 583–96.

iv   Rogers, F., & Head, B. (1983). *Mister Rogers talks with parents.* Berkley Books.

v   Bogost, I. (2018). The fetishization of Mr. Rogers's "Look for the helpers". *The Atlantic.*

vi   Foster, P.S., Smith, E.W.L. & Webster, D.G. (1999). The psychophysiological differentiation of actual, imagined and recollected anger. *Imagination, Cognition and Personality, 18*(3), 189–203.

vii   Foster, P.S., Webster, D.G. & Williamson, J. (2003). The psychophysiological differentiation of actual, imagined and recollected mirth. *Imagination, Cognition and Personality, 22*(2), 163–80.

viii   ABC News. (2018). Hangry is officially a word in the Oxford English Dictionary. *ABC News.*

ix   Orchant, R. (2013). 10 things hangry people do. *Huffpost.*

x   DeWall, C.N., Deckman, T., Gailliot, M.T. & Bushman, B. J. (2011). Sweetened blood cools hot tempers: Physiological self-control and aggression. *Aggressive Behavior, 37*(1), 73–80.

xi   Bushman, B.J., DeWall, C.N., Pond, R.S., Jr. & Hanus, M.D. (2014). Low glucose relates to greater aggression in married couples. *Proceedings of the National Academy of Sciences, 111*(17), 6254–7.

xii   Boon, M.E., van Hooff, M.L.M., Vink, J.M. & Geurts, S.A.E. (2023). The effect of fragmented sleep on emotion regulation ability and usage. *Cognition and Emotion, 37*(6), 1132–43.

xiii   Vandekerckhove, M. & Wang, Y. (2018). Emotion, emotion regulation and sleep: An intimate relationship. *AIMS Neuroscience, 5*(1), 1–17.

xiv   Mahindru, A., Patil, P. & Agrawal, V. (2023). Role of physical activity on mental health and well-being: A review. *Cureus, 15*(1), e33475.

xv   Pross, N., Demazières, A., Girard, N., Barnouin, R., Metzger, D., Klein, A., Perrier, E. & Guelinckx, I. (2014). Effects of changes in water intake on mood of high and low drinkers. *PloS One*, 9(4), e94754.

xvi   Jimenez, M.P., DeVille, N.V., Elliott, E.G., Schiff, J.E., Wilt, G.E., Hart, J.E. & James, P. (2021). Associations between nature exposure and health: A review of the evidence. *International Journal of Environmental Research and Public Health*, 18(9), 4790.

xvii   Bratman, G.N., Daily, G.C., Levy, B.J. & Gross, J.J. (2015). The benefits of nature experience: Improved affect and cognition. *Landscape and Urban Planning*, 138, 41–50.

xviii   Kaplan, R. & Kaplan, S. (1989). *The Experience of Nature: A Psychological Perspective*. New York: Cambridge University Press.

xix   Peterson, M.N., Larson, L.R., Hipp, A., Beall, J.M., Lerose, C., Desrochers, H., Lauder, S., Torres, S., Tarr, N.A., Stukes, K., Stevenson, K. & Martin, K.L. (2024). Birdwatching linked to increased psychological well-being on college campuses: A pilot-scale experimental study. *Journal of Environmental Psychology*, 96, 102306.

xx   Keyes, H., Gradidge, S., Forwood, S.E., Gibson, N., Harvey, A., Kis, E., Mutsatsa, K., Ownsworth, R., Roeloffs, S. & Zawisza, M. (2024). Creating arts and crafting positively predicts subjective wellbeing. *Frontiers in Public Health*, 12, 1417997.

xxi   Pesata, V., Colverson, A., Sonke, J., Morgan-Daniel, J., Schaefer, N., Sams, K., Carrion, F. M.-E. & Hanson, S. (2022). Engaging the arts for wellbeing in the United States of America: A scoping review. *Frontiers in Psychology*, 12, 791773.

xxii   Schwarz, N. & Clore, G.L. (1983). Mood, misattribution and judgments of well-being: Informative and directive functions of affective states. *Journal of Personality and Social Psychology*, 45(3), 513–23.

xxiii   Beck, A. T. (1967). *Depression: Causes and treatment*. Philadelphia: University of Pennsylvania Press.

xxiv   Martin, R.C. & Dahlen, E.R. (2011). Angry thoughts and response to provocation: Validity of the Angry Cognitions Scale. *Journal of Rational-Emotive and Cognitive Behavior Therapy*, 29(2), 65–76.

xxv   Martin, R.C. & Dahlen, E.R. (2007). The Angry Cognitions Scale: A new inventory for assessing cognitions in anger. *Journal of Rational-Emotive and Cognitive Behavior Therapy*, 25, 155–73.

xxvi   Chou, T., Deckersbach, T., Dougherty, D.D. & Hooley, J.M. (2023). The default mode network and rumination in individuals at risk for depression. *Social Cognitive and Affective Neuroscience*, 18(1).

xxvii   Martin, R. C. (2025). The Anger Project [Unpublished raw dataset]. University of Wisconsin-Green Bay, Green Bay.

xxviii Garnefski, N., Kraaij, V. & Spinhoven, P. (2001). Negative life events, cognitive emotion regulation and emotional problems. *Personality and Individual Differences*, 30(8), 1311–27.

xxix   Martin, R.C. & Dahlen, E.R. (2005). Cognitive emotion regulation in the prediction of depression, anxiety, stress and anger. *Personality and Individual Differences, 39*(7), 1249–60.

xxx Kuru, E., Safak, Y., Ozdemir, I., Tulaci, R.G., Ozdel., K., Ozkula, N.G. & Orsel., S. (2017). Cognitive distortions in patients with social anxiety disorder: Comparison of a clinical group and healthy controls. *European Journal of Psychiatry, 32*(2), 97–104.

xxxi Wood, J.V., Perunovic, W.Q.E. & Lee, J.W. (2009). Positive self-statements: Power for some, peril for others. *Psychological Science, 20*(7), 860–66.

xxxii Keltner, D. & Gross, J.J. (1999). Functional accounts of emotions. *Cognition & Emotion, 13*(5), 467–80.

xxxiii Berkovich-Ohana, A., Wilf, M., Kahana, R., Arieli, A. & Malach, R. (2015). Repetitive speech elicits widespread deactivation in the human cortex: The "mantra" effect? *Brain and Behavior, 5*(7), e00346.

xxxiv American Psychiatric Association. (2022). *Diagnostic and Statistical Manual of Mental Disorders* (5th ed., text rev.). Washington, D.C.: American Psychiatric Publishing.

xxxv Lithwick, D. (2012). Chaos Theory: A Unified Theory of Muppet Types. *Slate, 171.*

xxxvi Brockman, R., Ciarrochi, J., Parker, P. & Kashdan, T. (2017). Emotion regulation strategies in daily life: Mindfulness, cognitive reappraisal and emotion suppression. *Cognitive Behaviour Therapy, 46*(2), 91–113.

xxxvii Kross, E., Ayduk, Ö. & Mischel, W. (2005). When asking "why" does not hurt: Distinguishing rumination from reflective processing of negative emotions. *Psychological Science, 16*(9), 709–15.

xxxviii Kross, E. & Ayduk, Ö. (2011). Making meaning out of negative experiences by self-distancing. *Current Directions in Psychological Science, 20*(3), 187–91.

xxxix Zillman, D., Katcher, A.H. & Milavsky, B. (1972). Excitation transfer from physical exercise to subsequent aggressive behavior. *Journal of Experimental Social Psychology, 8*(3), 247–59.

xl Kjærvik, S.L. & Bushman, B.J. (2024). A meta-analytic review of anger management activities that increase or decrease arousal: What fuels or douses rage? *Clinical Psychology Review, 109,* 102414.

xli Niles, A.N., Haltom, K.E.B., Mulvenna, C.M., Lieberman, M.D. & Stanton, A.L. (2014). Randomized controlled trial of expressive writing for psychological and physical health: The moderating role of emotional expressivity. *Anxiety, Stress & Coping, 27*(1), 1–17.

xlii Baikie, K.A. & Wilhelm, K. (2005). Emotional and physical health benefits of expressive writing. *Advances in Psychiatric Treatment, 11*(5), 338–46.

xliii Speed, B.C., Goldstein, B.L. & Goldfried, M.R. (2018). Assertiveness training: A forgotten evidence-based treatment. *Clinical Psychology: Science and Practice, 25*(1), 1–20.

xliv Koch, S., Kunz, T., Lykou, S. & Cruz, R. (2014). Effects of dance movement therapy and dance on health-related psychological outcomes: A meta-analysis. *The Arts in Psychotherapy, 41*(1), 46–64.

xlv   Haeyen, S., van Hooren, S., van der Veld, W.M. & Hutschemaekers, G. (2018). Measuring the contribution of art therapy in multidisciplinary treatment of personality disorders: The construction of the Self-Expression and Emotion Regulation in Art Therapy Scale (SERATS). *Personality and Mental Health, 12*(1), 3–14.

xlvi   Haeyen, S., van Hooren, S., van der Veld, W.M. & Hutschemaekers, G. (2018). Measuring the contribution of art therapy in multidisciplinary treatment of personality disorders: The construction of the Self-Expression and Emotion Regulation in Art Therapy Scale (SERATS). *Personality and Mental Health, 12*(1), 3–14.

xlvii Haeyen, S., van Hooren, S., van der Veld, W.M. & Hutschemaekers, G. (2018). Measuring the contribution of art therapy in multidisciplinary treatment of personality disorders: The construction of the Self-Expression and Emotion Regulation in Art Therapy Scale (SERATS). *Personality and Mental Health, 12*(1), 3–14.

xlviii Haeyen, S., van Hooren, S., van der Veld, W.M. & Hutschemaekers, G. (2018). Measuring the contribution of art therapy in multidisciplinary treatment of personality disorders: The construction of the Self-Expression and Emotion Regulation in Art Therapy Scale (SERATS). *Personality and Mental Health, 12*(1), 3–14.

xlix   Cohen, S. & Wills, T.A. (1985). Stress, social support and the buffering hypothesis. *Psychological Bulletin, 98*(2), 310–57.

l   Van Zomeren, M., Spears, R., Fischer, A.H. & Leach, C.W. (2004). Put your money where your mouth is! Explaining collective action tendencies through group-based anger and group efficacy. *Journal of Personality and Social Psychology, 87*(5), 649–64.